The Irving B. Har
of the ZERO TO 1

Rachel Abramson, Ginger K. Breedlove, and Beth Isaacs are the winners of a 2003 Irving B. Harris Award of the ZERO TO THREE Press. Created by the late Irving B. Harris, these generous stipends offered essential support to outstanding authors for the development of book manuscripts that address issues of emerging importance to the multidisciplinary infant–family field. The ZERO TO THREE Press Editorial Board selected the recipients from among manuscripts submitted for consideration during five competitions in 2003 through 2005. *The Community-Based Doula: Supporting Families Before, During, and After Childbirth* is a result of Harris' generosity and belief in the power of books to make a lasting difference in the way we care for infants, toddlers, and families.

The Community-Based Doula: Supporting Families Before, During, and After Childbirth

Rachel Abramson • *Ginger K. Breedlove* • *Beth Isaacs*

ZERO TO THREE
Washington, DC

Published by

ZERO
TO
THREE®

ZERO TO THREE
2000 M St., NW, Suite 200
Washington, DC 20036-3307
(202) 638-1144
Toll-free orders (800) 899-4301
Fax: (202) 638-0851
Web: http://www.zerotothree.org

The mission of the ZERO TO THREE Press is to publish authoritative research, practical resources, and new ideas for those who work with and care about infants, toddlers, and their families. Books are selected for publication by an independent Editorial Board. The views contained in this book are those of the authors and do not necessarily reflect those of ZERO TO THREE: National Center for Infants, Toddlers and Families, Inc.

These materials are intended for education and training to help promote a high standard of care by professionals. Use of these materials is voluntary and their use does not confer any professional credentials or qualification to take any registration, certification, board or licensure examination, and neither confers nor infers competency to perform any related professional functions.

The user of these materials is solely responsible for compliance with all local, state or federal rules, regulations or licensing requirements. Despite efforts to ensure that these materials are consistent with acceptable practices, they are not intended to be used as a compliance guide and are not intended to supplant or to be used as a substitute for or in contravention of any applicable local, state or federal rules, regulations or licensing requirements. ZERO TO THREE expressly disclaims any liability arising from use of these materials in contravention of such rules, regulations or licensing requirements.

The views expressed in these materials represent the opinions of the respective authors. Publication of these materials does not constitute an endorsement by ZERO TO THREE of any view expressed herein, and ZERO TO THREE expressly disclaims any liability arising from any inaccuracy or misstatement.

Cover design and text design: Design Consultants, Inc.

Library of Congress Cataloging-in-Publication Data

Abramson, Rachel.
  The community-based doula : supporting families before, during, and
after childbirth / Rachel Abramson, Ginger K. Breedlove, and Beth Isaacs.
    p. cm.
  ISBN 1-934019-01-1
  1. Doulas. 2. Doulas--Illinois--Chicago. 3. Community-based family
services. 4. Community-based family services--Illinois--Chicago. I.
Breedlove, Ginger K. II. Isaacs, Beth. III. Title.
  RG950.A27 2006
  362.198'4500977311--dc22

                          2006028610

10 9 8 7 6 5 4 3 2 1
ISBN 1-934019-01-1
Printed in the United States of America

Suggested citation:
Abramson, R., Breedlove, G. K., & Isaacs, B. (2006). *The community-based doula: Supporting families before, during, and after childbirth*. Washington, DC: ZERO TO THREE.

Dedication

For Irving B. Harris, who walked upstream to make it happen.

And for Emily Fenichel, who *doula'ed* the telling of it.

Table of Contents

Foreword

This well-written, comprehensive book is about doulas—experienced women who help other women around the time of childbirth. *The Community-Based Doula: Supporting Families Before, During, and After Childbirth* is a gift to all who presently or in the future wish to help low-income pregnant teenagers and their newborns get off to a good start. The book describes Chicago Health Connection's organizational and operational experience assisting underserved, primarily African-American and Hispanic women in Chicago, before, during, and after childbirth.

The success of the community-based doula program has required the work of many skilled, innovative, and dedicated women and the cooperative efforts of several organizations with years of experience. The authors trace the beginnings of the community-based aspects of the current doula program to Chicago Health Connection's organizational predecessor, the Chicago Breastfeeding Task Force, which developed a widely recognized breastfeeding peer counselor training and support program in the mid-1980s. The program emphasized reinforcement of self-esteem and empowerment. It was interactive, participant-driven, and focused on personal and social change. When it became the lead agency for the Chicago Doula Project, Chicago Health Connection applied and adapted the focus on educational and personal development skills that had been learned from its earlier community-based work.

Irving Harris and the Chicago Doula Project

We can trace the origins of the doula project to a remarkably wise, generous, and persistent businessman, Irving Harris. After learning about exciting research in the 1970s that revealed the abilities of young infants, Irving Harris, at an age when most men are ready for retirement, started a new career. He participated regularly in the meetings of infant research pioneers, mainly developmental psychologists, child and adolescent psychiatrists, and pediatricians, where he learned about the importance of early mother–infant interaction and bonding. Using novel research methods, ingenious investigators discovered that newborn infants had many talents. For example, they could see and discriminate objects as long as they were located at approximately the distance between the eyes of the baby nursing at the breast and his mother's eyes. With this information, physicians and nurses could show parents that their baby could see, remember what they had seen, and indicate a preference for novel objects. These and other research discoveries gave new parents a fresh view and appreciation of their amazingly talented newborns.

Irving Harris was concerned about the plight of pregnant teenagers and the often very unfortunate outcomes awaiting them and their babies. He had been successful in business and applied the same energetic, thorough, and thoughtful approach that had worked for him in developing and promoting a product to helping low-income pregnant teenagers. Through his own generous financial support and his ability to persuade public officials of the effectiveness of new programs for these young women and their infants, Harris brought about an increase in the services for their care. But as he said to me years later, "No matter what we did, we always missed 10 to 15%" of pregnant teenagers." He indicated that this gap could be corrected with the addition of continuous doula support to home visiting and other programs for pregnant teens.

Early in the 1980s, pediatricians Marshall Klaus, Roberto Sosa, and I realized that our two studies in Guatemala had shown that if a woman (called a doula) stayed with a mother continuously through labor and delivery there would be striking benefits for the mother and her baby, compared to mothers laboring alone (Klaus, Kennell, Robertson, & Sosa, 1986; Sosa, Kennell, Klaus, Robertson, & Urrutia, 1980). In the United States, obstetricians were skeptical about these studies. We concluded that only a study in the United States might be considered valid. Funds provided by Irving Harris made that study possible; through that experience he learned about doulas. Unfortunately, we had to stop that study after a few months because of local hospital problems. Irving helped us with that decision. I did not hear from him for several years, but he had not forgotten about the doula. For years, he had, wisely, wanted to include doula support in a Chicago program for pregnant teenagers.

Chapter Three of this book is an inspirational resource for people who are considering starting a community doula program. The chapter describes the many ingredients, individuals, and community programs in Chicago that had long experience working with low-income pregnant and parenting teens before the community-based doula program began. On the basis of 10 years of experience in preparing peer counselors, Chicago Health Connection recognized the need for extensive lay health worker/doula training—60–70 hours of pre-service classroom time and subsequent monthly inservice training and discussion classes, along with reflective program supervision to nurture the doulas. The trained, experienced doulas whose stories enliven this book make it clear that the program's educational efforts have been successful and provide a model for other community doula programs.

Inspired by talking with doulas in Chicago, I think back to the very poor young women who participated in the two doula studies in Guatemala that revealed the power of doula support (Klaus, et al., 1986; Sosa, et al., 1980). These young women were approximately the same age as the Chicago teenagers. The young women in Guatemala and Illinois faced similar difficulties during their first pregnancies, labors and deliveries, and adjustment to motherhood and childrearing. But unlike the Guatemalan women, the Chicago teens, from the start of the Chicago Doula Project, had the support of their doula and all necessary assistance and support prenatally, perinatally, through the first year, and beyond.

Continuous Support During Childbirth

The following observations and speculations come from more than a quarter century of research studying the effects of continuous support by a doula. Approximately 5 million years ago, anatomical and behavioral changes started in the human that ultimately led to upright, bipedal walking. Between 400,000 and 500,00 years ago the changes in the human bony pelvis, plus the increasing size of the human brain and head resulted in a major change in the human baby's passage through the birth canal. Primate infants other than the human—such as chimpanzees—are born facing the mother so she can observe and remove any foreign matter on the face or move the umbilical cord from around the neck if it interferes with the descent of the baby or with the baby's airway. Our early human ancestors gave birth this way as well. However, as the pelvis of human mothers changed and the size of babies' heads increased, the human baby was now born facing away from the mother. For a mother alone, childbirth became more difficult and dangerous. The presence of another woman during the final stages of delivery may have made the difference between life and death for the mother and infant. The presence of one or more women at childbirth became a common human practice, probably for hundreds of thousands of years. A review of anthropologic data about birthing practices in 127 representative nonindustrialized societies reveals that in all but one, a woman provides support to the laboring mother (Klaus, Kennell, Berkowitz, & Klaus, 1992; Murdock & White, 1969). For example, Mayan Indians require that the woman's mother and a person or persons the mother knows well be with the laboring woman throughout her labor. In the United States, for the past century, birth has been moved into the hospital and away from this model.

To emphasize the value of a woman companion who is warm, supportive, and caring, we chose the Greek word "doula" for a lay woman caregiver who provides continuous physical, emotional, and informational support to the mother during labor and delivery. She "mothers the mother," an appropriate role for a doula who is continuously present with a woman in her teens. The doula uses her strength and confidence to relax the teenager, reduce her anxiety, and decrease her catecholamine levels.

Research Findings

During my pediatric career, two exciting and heart-warming experiences stand out. The first was when Drs. Marshall Klaus, Roberto Sosa, and I met to analyze the results, collected by our Guatemalan research workers, of our first study of continuous support for women during labor. The outcome for the supported mothers and their babies was significantly better, and supported mothers labored less than half as long as the routine care mothers (Sosa, et al., 1980).

The second experience occurred when I attended the meeting at which the results of the 4-year Chicago Doula Project were presented. Doula after doula told about her own desperate situation when she had found herself pregnant in her early teens—no one to help her, dropped out of school, suicidal, often no place to live. Yet a few years later, the doulas were happy, self-assured, enthusiastic about their work, and committed to helping pregnant teenagers. At that meeting, I also met many of the remarkable teachers and skilled supporters who found similarly desperate pregnant teenagers and prepared them for a successful birth and motherhood.

Above and beyond the benefits for the mother, the long–term advantage of doula support during labor may be even greater for the baby. In several of the randomized studies that we and others have conducted, mothers who have continuous doula support are more confident, and their feelings about their newborns are more positive, than the mothers who receive only routine care during childbirth (Hofmeyer, Nikodem, Wolman, Chalmers, & Kramer, 1991; Wolman, 1991). The doula-supported mothers said that they coped well during their labor and delivery, and that their babies were more beautiful, more clever, and easier to manage than a "standard" baby. They also said that their babies were better-than-average sleepers. These comments were markedly different from those of the routine-care mothers, who stated that their babies were slightly less beautiful and clever than a standard infant. More doula-supported mothers breastfed successfully, and they spent less time away from their babies in the first 6 weeks. In one study, doula mothers reported it took an average of 2.9 days to fall in love and "bond" with their babies, compared with 9.8 days for the routine-care mothers (Wolman, 1991). The continuous labor support of the mother by a doula appears to facilitate the doula-supported mothers' readiness to fall in love, bond with, and stay close to their babies.

In a carefully controlled randomized study, investigators visited doula-supported and routine-care mothers in their homes 2 months after delivery. The investigators did not know whether a mother had had a doula or not. Findings showed that doula-supported mothers had significantly more affectionate interactions with their infants than routine care mothers who had epidural or narcotic medication. There is good reason to speculate that the reactions and behavior of mothers who received continuous doula support are showing us the way mothers responded to their new baby for hundreds and thousands of years prior to the movement of labor and delivery into the hospital. Mothers' increased affectionate behavior and attention to the baby in the first 2 months of life may result in many more babies being securely attached to their mothers at 1 year, with all the desirable early and later outcomes associated with that designation.

Community-Based Doulas has been so inspirational, informative, and enjoyable for me that I hope it will be read by leaders in every community that has facilities and programs for teenagers and labor and delivery; every midwife and doula; and all supporters and advocates for mothers, babies, children, and adolescents. I don't think that it is possible to read this book without getting valuable ideas and inspiration.

Congratulations and thanks to Rachel, Ginger, and Beth. May this book and the inspiration of your success result in community-based doula programs throughout our country.

John H. Kennell, MD
Professor of Pediatrics Emeritus
Case Western Reserve University School of Medicine
Cleveland, Ohio

References

Hofmeyr, G. J., Nikodem, V. C., Wolman, W., Chalmers, B., & Kramer, T. (1991). Companionship to modify the clinical birth environment: Effects on progress and perceptions of labour, and breastfeeding. *British Journal of Obstetrics and Gynaecology, 98*, 756–764.

Klaus, M., Kennell, J., Berkowitz, G., & Klaus, P. (1992). Maternal assistance and support in labor: Father, nurse, midwife or doula? *Clinical Consultations in Obstetrics and Gynecology, 4,* 211–217.

Klaus, M., Kennell, J., Robertson, S., & Sosa, R. (1986). Effects of social support during parturition on maternal and infant morbidity. *British Medical Journal, 293,* 585–587.

Murdock, G. P., & White, D. R. (1969). Standard cross-cultural sample. *Ethology, 8,* 329–369.

Sosa, R., Kennell, J., Klaus, M., Robertson, S., & Urrutia, J. (1980). The effect of a supportive companion on perinatal problems: Length of labor, and mother-infant interaction. *The New England Journal of Medicine, 303,* 597–600.

Wolman, W. L. (1991). *Social support during childbirth: Psychological and physiological outcomes.* Unpublished masters thesis, University of Witwatersrand, Johannesburg, South Africa.

Acknowledgments

We must first acknowledge and honor the seminal work of those on whose shoulders we stand. The point of standing "on the shoulders of giants," as Sir Isaac Newton said, is that it allows you to see farther. We owe our perspective in the development of the community-based doula model to a great many original thinkers and courageous activists, but several in particular. Dana Raphael (1973) first formally described the support of women during and after childbirth and reclaimed the term *doula* for this role. Drs. John Kennell and Marshall Klaus published with Roberto Sosa and colleagues the first scientific studies documenting the effect of a supportive companion during labor and birth on rates of medical interventions and benefits to mother and baby (Klaus, Kennell, Robertson, & Sosa, 1986; Sosa, Kennell, Klaus, Robertson, & Urrutia, 1980). Their contributions focused attention on this ancient role and popularized the word doula in the medical community. We also owe a great debt of gratitude to Irving Harris, whose recognition of the revolutionary importance of the doula role moved him to push in every way possible to make this idea a reality for families who are underserved or who are alienated from established systems of care.

We are also indebted to our funders and partners in a 4-year pilot project called "The Chicago Doula Project." This project established the feasibility and the effectiveness of the community-based doula model in three grassroots settings serving teen parents from low-income communities. We are grateful to our initial funders, the Irving B. Harris Foundation and the Robert Wood Johnson Foundation's Local Initiatives Funding Partners Program, and to the Prince Charitable Trust, which enabled us to expand the project by adding additional doulas to some of the pilot sites. We were incredibly fortunate to partner with Alivio Medical Center, Christopher House, and Marillac Social Center, three organizations that serve their communities with creativity and dedication, and with the Ounce of Prevention Fund, which conducted the project evaluation.

The authors owe much to the staff and board of Chicago Health Connection, past and present, and to the countless doulas, home visitors, supervisors, and young parents who generously shared their experiences and their passion. In particular, we are grateful to the following doulas and project staff for teaching us and allowing us to use their words to describe the work: Ana Baro, Juana Burchell, Michele Fallon, Rosalba Felix, Lovie Griffin, Maureen Hallagan, Wandy Hernandez, Bina Holland, Earnestine Johnson, Bonnie Matty, Jeretha McKinley, Sandra Morales, Hao Nguyen, Judy Teibloom-Mishkin, Tikvah Wadley, Loretha Weisinger, and Tracy Wilhoite. Thanks go as well to friends, comrades, and allies who provided critical support and feedback and who read the manuscript: Susan Altfeld, Emily Fenichel, Phyllis Glink, Dr. Sydney Hans, Dr. Robert Harmon, Dr. Jon Korfmacher, Laura McAlpine, Mary McGonigel, Jeretha McKinley, Dr. Keith Packard, and Rebecca Shahmoon Shanok. Above all, we thank our families, who make life as sweet as it gets.

The authors come to this work from a number of perspectives. As women and mothers, we are acutely aware of birth as one of the essential human transitions—worthy of respect, dignity, and celebration. As practitioners in maternal–child health with a combined 75 years of experience of nursing practice, we know that birth is a powerful time of risk and opportunity. Working in support of families from underserved communities, we are determined to be involved in this time of potential growth, learning, and health.

We believe that community-based doulas do essential work. Being with another person in her time of need—standing firmly in one's own strength and helping the person in need find hers—is the ultimate human act. It is the essence of relationship-based work. Strong, caring relationships nurture babies, and these same positive relationships keep adults vital and learning. In nurturing that human potential, doulas expand their own potential as well. Thus, the community-based doula model is also a community development strategy. Building communities that stand together gives us hope for the future and is the most essential form of family support.

References

Klaus, M., Kennell, J., Robertson, S., & Sosa, R. (1986). Effects of social support during parturition on maternal and infant morbidity. *British Medical Journal*, 293, 585–587.

Raphael, D. (1973). *The tender gift: Breastfeeding*. New York: Schocken Books.

Sosa, R., Kennell, J., Klaus, M., Robertson, S., & Urrutia, J. (1980). The effect of a supportive companion on perinatal problems: Length of labor, and mother–infant interaction. *The New England Journal of Medicine*, 11, 597–600.

Introduction

This book is about doulas. The role of an experienced woman helping another woman around the time of childbirth is an ancient one. Quite possibly, this support was essential for human survival. As childbirth fell under the provenance of the medical profession and moved from the home to the hospital, this role was diminished and the idea of childbirth support fell out of favor. The revival of interest in natural childbirth in the 1960s was accompanied by a focus on childbirth support. Both the term *doula* and the role of a labor support provider were popularized in this country in the 1970s and 1980s.

In this book, we focus on community-based doulas, women who provide support during the childbearing year to other women within their community. We focus on Chicago Health Connection's community-based doula model as a new approach to supporting families from underserved communities. It is an intensive, strength-based intervention that can profoundly affect families who face difficult challenges.

Community-based doulas engage with pregnant women early in their pregnancy and continue to provide support into the early months of parenting. These doulas connect women and families to existing systems of care by developing trusting relationships with them. By design, these doulas are hired from the same neighborhoods and share the same culture, values, and language as the women and families they serve.

Our intention in this book is to describe the community-based doula model and to engage readers in thinking about the possibilities for this kind of work in their own agencies and communities. We hope to provide both a basis for reflection and a stimulus for action and to move readers to an active assessment of their particular settings. We have chosen to include in this volume both theoretical information and practical applications relevant to diverse audiences. We also incorporate the voices of community-based doulas and the women they serve to convey the richness of their shared experiences. One of our goals is to provide information and questions to stimulate local conversations about the unmet needs of birthing families—addressing both common themes and issues specific to individual communities and considering how the community-based doula model can be part of the solution.

We begin by describing in chapter 1 the history of the doula role and the literature on the effect of labor support. Chapter 2 gives the context of the community-based approach, tells the story of how Chicago Health Connection came to this work, describes the role of community-based providers in health promotion and social support, and discusses the literature on the effectiveness of paraprofessional home visitors and outreach workers. Chapter 3 is an overview of the community-based doula model and its essential components. Chapter 4 is a description of the Chicago Doula Project, a 4-year pilot project that developed and tested the community-based doula intervention. Chapter 5 focuses on recruitment, education, and support of doulas in the community-based doula model. We describe characteristics of promising doula recruits, their transition into the doula role, and the importance—in both theoretical and practical terms—of their training, as well as the critical importance of ongoing reflective supervision.

Chapter 6 incorporates the voices of community-based doulas. Doulas share their stories and perspectives on the personal meaning of their work, how it affects their lives, and how they experience the effect on their clients. Doulas and program administrators describe program challenges, difficult and inspiring moments, and the daily, incremental work of building relationships with clients and their families, creating a focus on the developing baby, and providing the nurturing touch at critical moments. These reflections highlight the richness of the experience for the doulas.

Chapter 7 explores the experience of women supported by doulas. Teen mothers who had doula support describe their experiences during pregnancy, birth, and the early postpartum period, with a focus on hope and goal-setting. These selections illustrate the mothers' perceptions of the profoundly important effect of doula support. One teen explained, "They done told me to strive for what I want to strive for and, no matter what, let no one take my hopes and my dreams away from me. No one ever encouragin' me like that before" (Breedlove, 2001, p. 75).

Chapter 8 focuses on the practicalities of replicating the community-based doula model, including finding a community that really needs and wants this intervention, developing a local community assessment, building a collaborative initiative, and creating a plan that adapts the model to meet local objectives and make use of local resources while maintaining fidelity to its key principles.

We conclude with an examination in chapter 9 of the broader context of emerging community-based doula practice and a call to action in chapter 10.

Implementing the community-based doula model is challenging on a number of levels. Incorporating intensive support around childbirth into ongoing social support programs can be complicated. Integrating a long-term home visiting model with medical and nursing care in the hospital also comes with political and practical challenges. The profound effect of the model on mothers, infants, and families is worth the considerable effort it takes to overcome these challenges. Making a difference in the lives of families takes engaging and supporting them in the ways that make the most sense to them.

The past decade has brought unassailable scientific support to the understanding that early experiences affect human development. The new research on brain development, highlighted in the landmark 2000 report *From Neurons to Neighborhoods: The Science of Early Childhood Development* (National Research Council & Institute of Medicine, 2000) makes it clear that brain cells begin learning during fetal development. Advances in neurobiology show us changes in the brains of infants and mothers alike in response to stress and trauma and in response to each other. Therefore, what happens to women during pregnancy, birth, and the early months of parenting is critically important. It matters for the baby's development, the mother's development, and the growth of the parent–child relationship.

The community-based doula model uniquely captures this period of sensitivity in a directed intervention for underserved populations that makes use of the power of mutual, trusting, and nurturing relationships over time. The doula nurtures the mother and her family so that they will connect to and nurture the baby.

References

Breedlove, G. K. (2001). *A description of social support and hope in pregnant and parenting teens receiving care from a doula.* Doctoral dissertation, University of Missouri—Kansas City. (UMI No. 3043597)

National Research Council & Institute of Medicine. (2000). *From neurons to neighborhoods: The science of early childhood development.* J. P. Shonkoff & D. A. Phillips, (Eds), Board on Children, Youth, and Families; Commission on Behavioral and Social Sciences and Education. Washington, DC: National Academy Press.

Chapter 1

Doulas and the Evidence Base for Birthing Support

The evolution of the word *doula* reflects an early understanding that women need other women to care for them during the childbearing years. The first use of the word *doula* can be traced to ancient Greece, where it was used to refer to a female servant. Then *doula* came to mean a woman who served and cared for the woman of the house, whose primary role was childbearing. Today, a doula is an experienced woman who supports another woman around the time of childbirth.

This chapter outlines the history of the doula role and describes doulas in the United States today, reviews the literature on the effect of labor support, and introduces the community-based doula model.

The Modern Doula

How did the term *doula* become modernized and incorporated into today's culture? The earliest published use of this word can be found in the book *The Tender Gift: Breastfeeding* (Raphael, 1973). American anthropologist Dana Raphael described the necessity of supportive care for mothers around pregnancy and childbirth in order to achieve successful breastfeeding. Raphael introduced the term *doula* to define a person who would provide support in early mothering, which she described as "mothering the mother." For Raphael, the doula, or designated caregiver, was any person (female or male) who assisted and eased the mother through her most acute childbearing and childrearing needs, referring primarily to postpartum support. Raphael's anthropological perspective focused on the need for sufficiency of human support during the childbearing and child-rearing process. She posited that sufficient support is a requirement for a new mother to achieve successful breastfeeding, confident attachment to her baby, and ease of transition into successful parenting.

At the same time that Raphael was promoting the concept of mothering the mother, noted pediatric researchers in the field of mother–infant bonding, John Kennell, Mary Anne Trause, and Marshall Klaus (1975), began to explore the significance of the period immediately after birth, which they called a "sensitive period." They suggested that during this "getting-to-know-you" time immediately after birth, the mother and infant should be observed, but left alone and encouraged to discover one another without interruption.

These researchers were curious as to whether a mother who actively participated in labor and birth, and then had an immediate opportunity to have and hold her infant, would demonstrate enhanced maternal attachment. In a 1975 study, they compared the behavior of 22 women who experienced conventional hospital births in Guatemalan and U. S. hospitals with that of women who gave birth at their homes in California. They filmed the mothers during the first minutes of contact with their naked newborns and found that home-birth mothers who were active birth participants immediately picked up their babies at birth, stroked the infants' faces, and started to breastfeed within minutes of delivery. Mothers who gave birth with conventional hospital interventions touched their infants less.

Foundational Research

While exploring the effect of the conditions surrounding birth, Klaus and Kennell began to wonder whether the presence of supportive companions during childbearing could affect outcomes of the mother or newborn. The first study to investigate this question, conducted by Roberto Sosa, John Kennell, Marshall Klaus, Steven Robertson, and J. J. Urrutia, was published in 1980. This research is foundational to the hypothesis that constant human support to women in labor provides significant, measurable perinatal benefits. Their work also provided a formal use of the term *doula* in reference to labor support, which introduced the term to a wider medical community through publication of the study in the *New England Journal of Medicine* (Sosa et al., 1980).

In this study, conducted in Guatemala, 127 normal, healthy laboring mothers were assigned to a control group or a doula-supported group. Labor support was provided by two women who had not previously met the laboring mothers. Supportive care consisted of physical contact (e.g., back rubs, holding hands), conversation, and friendly companionship. The authors found that the length of time from admission to birth was shorter for women who were assigned a doula compared with the length of time for women who labored alone. In addition, the likelihood of medical interventions in labor was less, mothers who had a doula were reported to have been awake more after delivery, and mothers with a doula were reported to smile at and talk to their babies more. The study sparked a surge of interest in conducting scientific research to investigate the effect of support during labor.

The Immediate and Long-Term Effect of Labor Support

As investigations continued to show an effect on perinatal outcomes, Klaus and Kennell (1983) postulated that doula support could rehumanize birthing practice in an increasingly technological and medically controlled environment. They hypothesized that labor support may be a protective factor during a vulnerable transition in life.

Returning to Guatemala, Klaus, Kennell, Robertson, and Sosa (1986) expanded the scope of their initial pilot study and recruited 465 healthy first-time mothers who arrived in labor at the local public hospital. Mothers were assigned to two groups: the control group (*n* = 249), or the experimental group (*n* = 168) who received the doula intervention. The intervention consisted of continuous emotional and physical support by one of three Guatemalan laywomen with no obstetric training. Support was given from admission to delivery, including routine usual care, and the laboring mothers were told they would never be left alone. Mothers in the control group received routine hospital care, which did not include consistent support. Study results suggested a reduction in labor length and use of Pitocin (labor induction or augmentation medication) and fewer problems associated with the infant for mothers supported in the doula group. This study documented the benefit of constant support to women during labor and suggested that supportive care may influence physiological processes in childbirth.

International interest continued to grow, and research emerged to investigate various supportive caregiver roles in labor and birth settings around the world. Gates Justus Hofmeyr and his colleagues conducted a randomized clinical trial at a hospital caring for low-income women in South Africa to determine whether support by a trained volunteer laywoman affected birth outcomes compared with intermittent care by staff on a busy hospital ward where husbands and family were not permitted (Hofmeyr, Nikodem, Wolman, Chalmers, & Kramer, 1991). This study found that continuous labor support had significant benefits, some of them long term. Women reported significantly less labor pain, required less analgesia, and expressed a greater sense of positive coping during labor. In addition, supported women were significantly more likely to breastfeed successfully and exclusively and to use a more flexible approach to feeding times. Other findings with a potentially profound effect were a decreased likelihood of postpartum depression and anxiety and greater self-esteem and confidence in mothering.

In another South African study, Wendy-Lynn Wolman, Beverly Chalmers, G. Justus Hofmeyr, and V. Cheryl Nikodem (1993) also examined the effect of doula support on postpartum depression. They conducted a randomized trial in which 92 of 189 first-time mothers were assigned a doula in a community hospital. Results showed higher self-esteem scores and lower postpartum depression and anxiety ratings in women who had doula support in labor. More recent related research has shown that the fetuses of mothers who were depressed or stressed exhibited different responses, including increases in heart rates, when compared with those of mothers who were emotionally healthy (Tarkan, 2004). These preliminary studies also reveal a greater risk for infants of depressed or stressed mothers to develop problems in learning and behavior and possibly an increased risk for anxiety or depression as they grow. Tarkan also described evidence that pregnant women who experience high levels of stress are likelier to deliver low-birthweight or preterm infants. A link between the pregnant mother's emotional state and her infant's subsequent emotional well-being and behavior implies that intervention by doulas during the pregnancies of vulnerable women may have positive outcomes for their children's development.

In 1998, Ana Langer and colleagues implemented a randomized controlled trial involving 724 women admitted for delivery in a large public hospital in Mexico City. The women in the study either received supportive care from a doula or were randomized into a usual-care group (Langer, Campero, Garcia, & Reynolds, 1998). They concluded that psychosocial support was associated with increased breastfeeding and shorter duration of labor.

Klaus and Kennell (1997) published a meta-analysis combining the results of 11 randomized clinical trials conducted throughout the world to examine outcomes of supportive care by doulas for healthy women having first births. A meta-analysis is an analysis of the available literature about a topic, ideally a synthesis of randomized trials, to arrive at a single summary statement of outcomes. Significant findings within all studies included a reduction in the duration of labor, less use of medication for labor pain relief, fewer forceps deliveries, and a reduction in cesarean sections. In one of the studies (Hofmeyr et al., 1991), researchers observed the psychological health of the mother and baby and found that mothers from the doula group had significantly less anxiety and higher breastfeeding rates at 6 weeks, compared with the no-doula group.

Comprehensive research conducted over decades by Kennell, Klaus, and others not only confirmed benefits in perinatal (labor, birth, and the immediate newborn period) outcomes but also demonstrated growing evidence of immediate and longer term mother–infant benefits. Mothers who had continuous labor support more frequently demonstrated increased alertness after birth, communicated more with their babies after birth, breastfed more, and reported less postpartum depression. Additionally, mothers' feelings of competence in labor (a sense of control and positive perception of the birth) were increased when they had labor support. That sense of mastery enhanced a woman's ongoing feeling of competence as a mother and her confidence in successful breastfeeding. Women who received continuous supportive care in labor were more likely to initiate breastfeeding and had fewer breastfeeding problems (Hofmeyr, et al.,1991; Scott, Klaus, & Klaus, 1999). Appendix A is an overview of studies in table form, with evidence of significance listed for five outcome categories.

Doula Research Today

Ellen Hodnett, Simon Gates, G. Justus Hofmeyr, and Carol Sakala published in 2003 in *The Cochran Journal* the most recent, comprehensive, systematic review of continuous support for women during childbirth. They reviewed studies of randomized controlled trials that assessed outcomes of mothers and infants who had continuous care during labor and delivery. Findings from 15 trials involving over 12,000 women in 11 countries are included in this meta-analysis. All trials involved one-on-one birthing support by women who were experienced through nursing, midwifery, or childbirth education, or through giving birth themselves. In general, the benefits of continuous labor support were divided into five outcome categories:

- *Labor*, such as use of Pitocin augmentation, epidural anesthesia, and effect on labor length;

- *Birth* outcomes or interventions, such as cesarean, vaginal, or operative (forceps/vacuum), and episiotomy;

- *Newborn* events, such as APGAR, admission to nursery type, breastfeeding;

- *Immediate psychological outcomes* of the mother, such as perception of the birth experience, stress in labor, and control during labor; and

- *Longer term maternal and infant* outcomes, such as postpartum depression, maternal self-esteem in the postpartum period, duration of breastfeeding, and difficulty mothering.

The studies included in the meta-analysis looked at a variety of settings and included a range of labor support roles. Outcomes of the studies were also variable, but it was possible to arrive at a number of broad conclusions. These included the following:

- Continuous labor support enhances the physiologic process of labor and enhances maternal confidence, which in turn, reduces the frequency of medical intervention.

- Effects appear to be stronger when the provider of support is not a member of the hospital staff and when support is begun early in labor.

- Emotional support, advocacy, and comfort measures reduce maternal anxiety and fear in labor, thereby reducing a potential chemical stress response effect in labor. A calmer, more confident mother less frequently experiences complications of labor such as abnormal fetal heart rate patterns, inefficient uterine contractility, and extended progress of labor.

- One-on-one labor support can reduce the cascade of medical interventions after epidural administration for pain management in labor, thus decreasing maternal and newborn morbidity associated with epidurals.

- Continuous support in labor can positively influence a mother's satisfaction with the childbirth experience.

Continuous labor support in the studies included in the meta-analysis encompassed support from a variety of caregivers, who differed in their experience, qualifications, and relationship to the women. Support was provided by nurses, midwives, student midwives, husbands, women with and without special training, and strangers. However, in all cases, the form of care evaluated was continuous presence and support from active labor through delivery in hospital settings. The effects of the different kinds of support providers were described as follows:

- The positive perinatal effects of continuous support included a reduction in maternal use of analgesia/anesthesia, increased rate of spontaneous vaginal birth, reduction in rate of operative vaginal birth (forceps, vacuum), and reduction in the rate of cesarean birth.

- There was no significant difference in maternal satisfaction with the childbirth experience related to labor support provided by staff members or nonstaff members.

- A dose–response phenomenon was demonstrated. Continuous labor support appears to be more effective when initiated early in labor, compared with support not initiated until active labor begins or later. Support also was more effective when provided by nonemployed caregivers and by women whose exclusive focus was labor support.

Hodnett and her colleagues (2003) concluded:

Given the clear benefits and no known risks associated with intrapartum support, every effort should be made to ensure that all labouring women receive support, not only from those close to them, but also from specially trained caregivers. This support should include continuous presence, the provision of hands-on comfort, and encouragement (p.14).

Doulas in the United States Today

The number of doulas in North America is growing each year, with the current doula estimate at 10,000–12,000. Membership in Doulas of North America (DONA), an organization that trains and certifies doulas, has grown from 750 in 1994 to 5,221 in 2005 (Doulas of North America, n.d.). Additionally, a number of other organizations train and certify doulas.

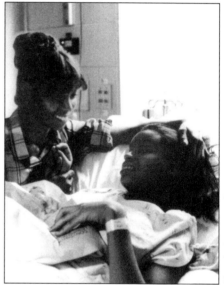

Photo by Nancy Pinzke

Today, doulas in the United States typically are trained lay attendants who accompany mothers during labor and birth, providing continuous presence and support. Birth doulas help women draft a birth plan and then offer them support during labor and the first few hours after birth. In a related role, postpartum doulas now provide a reassuring mix of motherly advice and hands-on assistance with everything from breastfeeding to cooking during the days and weeks after birth. A majority of doulas practicing in the United States charge a fee for their services and are employed directly by families.

The professional doula recognizes birth and motherhood as key life experiences. Doulas do not take the place of family support in labor or assume nursing or medical responsibilities. A doula provides physical support for the mother and emotional support for the mother and the family. She does not promote conflict with patient care recommendations or become directly involved with delivery of health care services. Doulas complement the functions of nurses and doctors, and work collaboratively in such a way that enhances the experience of childbirth. A fundamental principle emphasized in doula training is the scope and limits of practice. Doulas understand that their role is to educate the client and encourage her to speak on her own behalf—to find her own voice. It is the doula's role to inform clients of their choices, encourage them to ask questions—but not to directly confront nurses or doctors. In general, doulas encourage mothers to be active participants in labor, support nonpharmacological alternative therapies for pain management, promote immediate contact with the newborn, and support early initiation of breastfeeding.

Thus, the doula role has evolved from the highly regarded handmaiden of ancient Greece, to Raphael's modernized definition of a caring person "mothering the mother," to the modern doula who provides services, often for a fee, in the prenatal, labor, and postpartum periods. The doula has emerged as a significant contributor to improved labor and delivery outcomes for women. Just as important, the doula has demonstrated a significant effect on increasing breastfeeding rates, improving early mother–infant relationships, and enhancing maternal self-esteem.

The Community-Based Doula Model

The disparities in health care between those who have access to resources and those who do not have an enormous, life-long effect on maternal and child health. Throughout the United States, a growing number of childbearing women need supportive care in pregnancy, birth, and parenting but lack access to adequate services. They may have insufficient support from family and friends because of immigration, social isolation, or difficult family lives. Women in such circumstances typically are uninsured or on state public health insurance plans and cannot pay privately for doula services. These mothers often anticipate childbirth without the support they need and may face additional life challenges, including poverty, teen pregnancy, language barriers, or violence. What is at stake in these communities is nothing less than the future of the next generation.

The community-based doula model emerged to respond to the particular needs of such childbearing families. The model acknowledges the importance of cultural context in childbirth and is based on the assumption that support and care from women within a similar culture and community are empowering for pregnant and birthing women and positively affect the strength of the community. Community-based doulas tend to stay in the communities where they have worked, continuing their support of families on a professional and personal level and becoming neighborhood resources and community assets.

As in Raphael's description, doulas working in the community-based model are women serving women in their own communities, engaged in one-on-one relationships throughout pregnancy and over an extended period of time. This model extends the intensive, intimate support during birth into a long-term, trusting, supportive relationship with a pregnant woman and her family, which encourages strong connections and ultimately helps to build a nurturing environment for the newborn. The model makes the best use of the powerful time around birth to engage underserved families in an ongoing framework of support that optimizes outcomes for the mother and baby.

We will discuss the community-based doula model in great detail in later chapters, but first let's look at some context for community-based work in general.

References

Doulas of North America. (n.d.). *Statistics*. Retrieved May 27, 2005, from http://www.dona.org/Statistics.html

Hodnett, E. D., Gates, S., Hofmeyr, G. J., & Sakala, C. (2003). Continuous support for women during childbirth. *The Cochrane Database of Systematic Reviews, Issue 3* (Art. No. CD003766).

Hofmeyr, G. J., Nikodem, V., Wolman, W., Chalmers, B., & Kramer, T. (1991). Companionship to modify the clinical birth environment: Effects on progress and perceptions of labour, and breastfeeding. *British Journal of Obstetrics and Gynaecology, 98*, 756–764.

Kennell, J., Trause, M. A., & Klaus, M. (1975). Evidence for a sensitive period in the human mother. *Ciba Found Symposia, 33*, 87–101.

Klaus, M., & Kennell, J. (1983). Parent to infant bonding: Setting the record straight. *Journal of Pediatrics, 102*, 575–576.

Klaus, M., & Kennell, J. (1997). The doula: An essential ingredient of childbirth rediscovered. *Acta Paediatr, 86*, 1034–1036.

Klaus, M., Kennell, J., Robertson, S., & Sosa, R. (1986). Effects of social support during parturition on maternal and infant morbidity. *British Medical Journal, 293*, 585–587.

Langer, A., Campero, L., Garcia, C., & Reynolds, S. (1998). Effects of psychosocial support during labour and childbirth on breastfeeding, medical interventions, and mothers' well-being in a Mexican public hospital: A randomized clinical trial. *British Journal of Obstetrics and Gynaecology, 105*, 1056–1063.

Raphael, D. (1973). *The tender gift: Breastfeeding.* New York: Schocken Books.

Scott, K., Klaus, P., & Klaus, M. (1999). The obstetrical and postpartum benefits of continuous support during childbirth. *Journal of Women's Health & Gender-Based Medicine, 8*, 1257–1264.

Sosa, R., Kennell, J., Klaus, M., Robertson, S., & Urrutia, J. (1980). The effect of a supportive companion on perinatal problems: Length of labor, and mother–infant interaction. *The New England Journal of Medicine, 11*, 597–600.

Tarkan, L. (2004, December 7). Tracking stress and depression back to the womb. *New York Times.* Retrieved June 20, 2005, from http://deccanherald/dec202004/snt5.asp

Wolman, W., Chalmers, B., Hofmeyr, G. J., & Nikodem, V. C. (1993 Postpartum depression and companionship in the clinical birth environment: A randomized, controlled study. *American Journal of Obstetrics and Gynecology, 168*, 1388–1393.

Chapter 2

Community-Based Work: Doulas in Context

The origins of Chicago Health Connection (CHC) and the inspiration for our doula work were in a breastfeeding promotion program focused on low-income communities. CHC was a volunteer-driven effort around a number of kitchen tables in the mid-1980s, forming a group called the Chicago Breastfeeding Task Force. Our approach was an infant mortality reduction strategy, promoting breastfeeding in low-income Chicago communities where breastfeeding rates were low and infant mortality and morbidity rates were as high as those in developing countries. The coalition was a broad one and attracted parents, providers of maternal and child health care, and community advocates.

This chapter tells the story of how CHC came to this work, describes the role of community-based providers in health promotion and social support, and discusses the literature on the effectiveness of paraprofessional home visitors and outreach workers, all in the context of community-based doula work.

The Chicago Breastfeeding Task Force

From the beginning, the Chicago Breastfeeding Task Force focused on identifying the natural leadership that already existed within communities to promote maternal and child health. The health providers in the group—who were mostly nurses, nutritionists, and health educators—had a shared awareness of the intimate nature of infant feeding choices. We experienced firsthand the limits of what professionals can do to influence community norms and cultural expectations in such personal areas of health. We knew that medical information alone was not enough to support a decision to breastfeed in communities with few breastfeeding role models. We knew that the messenger is as important as the message and that the advice of a trusted family member, friend, or peer is sometimes much more powerful than information from a nurse or doctor or dietician. We fully understood that breastfeeding success requires long-term support, support that at the time was rarely available or accessible in underserved communities.

Peer Counselors

Consequently, our first funded project, which was supported by a grant from the March of Dimes, was the Breastfeeding Peer Counselor Program at Cook County Hospital, at the time Chicago's only public hospital (Kistin, Abramson, & Dublin, 1994). The program still exists as a continuing collaboration between what is now CHC and the John H. Stroger, Jr., Hospital of Cook County (formerly Cook County Hospital) Perinatal Center. Working at Cook County Hospital was a radical education for us on many levels. We learned that creating change in any large institution requires community-organizing techniques: learning the culture of the place, finding allies, building support, and continually re-evaluating and refining the effort. In a hospital, that means asking the professional health care providers what they think and engaging them in the change effort. Before training peer counselors, we first had to convene doctors, nurses, midwives, and administrators; develop policies; fight for resources for the program; and provide continuing education.

But, most of all, we learned from the peer counselors themselves, women whom we recruited from the postpartum wards at Cook County Hospital. These women were good at advocating for themselves and for others. Many had faced and overcome difficult life circumstances and, in the process, had developed significant skills, capacities, and wisdom. Some had suffered trauma and loss and used those experiences to motivate and inform their commitment to helping other women through difficulties.

Community-Based Training

Before we held our first training, our energized, inspired coalition had developed the longest, most detailed, and painstakingly and lovingly crafted breastfeeding training outline ever created. However, once Peg Dublin, the first coordinator of the program, began to train the first peer counselors, we tossed the curriculum out the window. We found that it was not effective to approach community-based training with fixed assumptions and a rigid agenda.

Our first training participants—strong natural leaders chosen for their energy and commitment—told us in words and by their actions that they would learn what they needed to know in the order and format that best fit their experience, their priorities, and their burning issues. Our initial well-intentioned breastfeeding lectures were constantly interrupted with questions about other pressing topics, and the conversations frequently strayed to issues the women were dealing with: violence in the home and in the community, financial pressures, parenting, and the health of their children.

We were taught principles of popular education, first by our training participants and later by the theories of Paulo Freire and practitioners of empowerment education (see chapter 5). We began to see that training for change begins with personal awareness and connects to a more political analysis, or "critical consciousness" (Eng, Salmon, & Mullan, 1992), and then moves in a structured path toward action. This is, in its essence, an empowerment model, which Eng and colleagues define as a "transformation process" (p. 5), by which people are supported in recognizing their own power to take action in their lives.

Focus on Relationships

We also learned from the breastfeeding peer counselors that our work was not only an infant-focused health promotion strategy but also fundamentally a woman-to-woman support model. Peer counselors showed us that the relationships they developed with their clients were as important as the breastfeeding information they shared. The work of developing that trusting connection was personally demanding and took considerable time and effort. They also taught us that their work with clients could not be limited to breastfeeding promotion. Once they developed personal connections, they became the trusted sources of information and support about multiple health and social issues. These peer counselors were the front-line contacts for help and referrals to resources and services in the face of family illness, emergency needs for food or housing, or the experience of community and family violence. Their work was holistic, longitudinal, and dependent on personal relationships, and they constantly pushed us to train them more broadly and expand their roles so they could better serve the families in their communities. Sometimes these relationships lasted for years, long after the formal peer counselor–client relationship ended.

The wisdom of these women and the profound effect they have had on families over the years guided the development of CHC's community-based doula model. They demonstrated to us how long it takes to develop trust with women who have had little to trust in their lives. They showed us the incredible openness to change of mothers and babies in the period surrounding birth. They illustrated the empowering effect of respectful engagement, and especially the power that comes from success in supporting another person's growth. The peer counselors nurtured the nurturers and mothered the mothers (as Dana Raphael, Marshall Klaus, and John Kennel have described), to help those mothers become responsive, emotionally available parents who felt proud of themselves and of their babies.

Becoming CHC

The Chicago Breastfeeding Task Force responded over time to the leadership of the peer counselors. We expanded the breastfeeding peer counselor training from 6 to 10 sessions to include nutrition, parenting, child development, and well-child care. We began to engage in other community health promotion efforts, and we developed a network for personal and professional support of the peer counselors.

After a year of strategic thinking and planning, in 1995 we expanded our organizational mission, changed our name to Chicago Health Connection (CHC) and broadened our work. Breastfeeding support was still central to our mission, but we found other maternal and child health issues that fit the mother-to-mother support model. We were involved in citywide immunization promotion, lead prevention, and some asthma support. We tried a number of strategies to broaden the breastfeeding peer counselor role into a more holistic, less restricted perinatal support role. Peer counselors—and, increasingly, our team members—were convinced that we needed to be present with women at birth if we were to profoundly affect their perinatal outcomes and their experiences as parents.

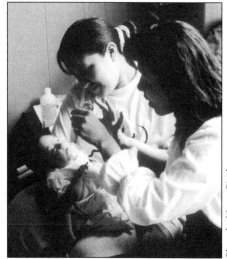

Photo by Nancy Pinzke

The Context—the Community Health Worker (CHW) Model

CHC was not doing this work in a vacuum. Our learning in Chicago paralleled other similar woman-to-woman support efforts in this country. La Leche League International began in the 1950s as a peer-to-peer breastfeeding support program, primarily in White, middle-class communities. Family support programs have grown in the United States since the 1970s, and Resource Mothers programs developed in southeastern states in the 1980s. By the early 1990s, peer counselor, community health advisor, and promotora (or health promoter) programs, were proliferating in a variety of settings. Lay health workers were being incorporated into health care teams to prevent and manage chronic illness, including HIV/AIDS, cancer, diabetes, and heart disease.

This work also took place in a broader international context. Developing countries have long used public health approaches that make use of lay health workers. The World Health Organization and the United Nations Children's Fund (UNICEF) described this role in the context of a primary health care (PHC) model in the Declaration of Alma-Ata, written at the 1978 International Conference on Primary Health Care in Alma-Ata, then the capital of the Kazakh Soviet Socialist Republic. Principles of PHC included equitable distribution of health resources, community participation "in the spirit of self-reliance and self-determination" (World Health Organization, 1978, p. 16), a focus on prevention, the use of technology appropriate to the socioeconomic environment, and collaboration across sectors of society, both public and private. Particularly interesting in the light of our work was the Declaration's statement about traditional birth attendants:

> Traditional medical practitioners and birth attendants are found in most societies. They are often part of the local community, culture, and traditions and continue to have high social standing in many places, exerting considerable influence on local health practices. With the support of the formal health system, these indigenous practitioners can become important allies in organizing efforts to improve the health of the community (World Health Organization, 1978, p. 63).

Similar approaches have been used in the United States since the 1950s, training layworkers from targeted communities to promote health, support families, and link underserved communities to health and social services (Rosenthal, 1998). This outreach role was mandated in the federal Migrant Health Act of 1962 and the Economic Opportunity Act of 1964 (Hill, Bone, & Butz, 1996). In 1968, the Indian Health Service formalized the use of Community Health Representatives in tribally managed or Indian Health Service programs.

The effectiveness of these "natural leaders" is based on the shared experience, language, and culture with the communities they serve and on decreased social distance, an increased ease of identification between provider and client. In addition, community health workers (CHWs) possess specific skills and capacities essential to creating trust and developing supportive relationships. CHWs are defined as community members who educate and serve individuals and groups to gain greater control over their health and their lives (Koch & Thompson, 1997). The CHW is a community insider who is employed in a formal role that transforms her community. The successful effect of CHWs on changing health behaviors has been attributed to the creation and strengthening of a network of social support (Roman, Lindsay, Moore, & Shoemaker, 1999).

An increased use of this approach in the late 1980s and a number of efforts during the 1990s to define and evaluate the CHW role have focused both academic and policy interest in this area. The National Community Health Advisor Study of 1998 estimated that there were at least 600 programs at that time, employing approximately 12,500 CHWs (Rosenthal, 1998).

Many of these programs developed in grassroots and underfunded settings, and the status of CHW outcome evaluation reflects that reality. Swider (2002) surveyed the database literature on CHW effect and found preliminary support for CHW effectiveness in increasing access to health care services, particularly in underserved populations. A smaller number of studies documented positive outcomes in the areas of increased health knowledge, improved health status outcomes, and behavioral changes, but the outcomes of these studies needed to be replicated in order to demonstrate conclusive results. Since that survey, there has been a growing literature supporting the effectiveness of CHWs in prevention and management of diabetes, cardiovascular disease, and breast cancer, sometimes with significant associated cost savings (Fedder, Chang, Curry, & Nichols, 2003). Nevertheless, there is still a need for a research agenda that clearly defines interventions, standardizes outcome measures, and documents cost-effectiveness.

Community-based (or paraprofessional) providers also have long been used in family support and home visiting programs (Hans & Korfmacher, 2002). Evaluations of program outcomes, as with health-focused programs, show mixed results (Daro & Harding, 1999; Duggan et al., 1999; Olds et al., 2002). Most research did not link program process outcomes with program participant outcomes, aside from quantity of home visits completed, topics addressed in home visits, and referrals made. Thus, it failed to identify program issues that might affect the quality and extent of program implementation compared to program designs (Duggan et al., 1999). One well-recognized study documented minimal effectiveness of paraprofessional home visitors as compared with nurses (Olds et al., 2002). This randomized controlled study evaluated a paraprofessional home visitor component of a program model designed for nurses, without substantially adapting the program model to the different strengths and challenges of the paraprofessional role (Olds et al., 2002).

Gaps in the literature around effectiveness of paraprofessional home visitors, similar to gaps in the CHW literature, limit our knowledge about what distinguishes paraprofessional programs that work from those with disappointing results. Describing CHW programs, Sue Swider notes that "the role can be doomed by overly high expectations, lack of a clear focus, and lack of documentation" (Swider, 2002, p. 19). The same can be said for paraprofessional home visitor programs. There is a particular need for research that explores the effect of program commitment to high-quality training, supervision, and support of paraprofessional family support workers (Hans & Korfmacher, 2002).

Community-Based Doulas

This community-based, relationship-based approach has demonstrated the potential for profound effect on birth and parenting outcomes. The meaning of birth is colored by both personal and cultural factors. The context and meaning of childbirth and parenting are intimate and communal, and affect parents' lives, children's lives, and perhaps generations to come.

Health and parenting education models typically have assumed that health care professionals hold important information, which, when given to consumers, result in healthy life choices. However, families and family systems are much more complicated than that. More recently, health promotion and family support programs have questioned the idea that families rely only on information from experts and have focused more on the influence of friends, family, and other peer or kindred networks on decision making in health and parenting behaviors.

The community-based doula can occupy the gap between the expert professionals in the health and human service systems and families whose life experiences keep them distant from resources and slow to trust. Understanding community context, and interpreting across cultural divides, the community-based doula plays a bridging role in helping families access important services and act on behalf of their own health.

Fragmentation and Continuity

Birth is the moment when our fabric of support for families is most torn. Not that we don't provide good services—there are many strong prenatal outreach and support programs and myriad services in the early postpartum period. Many hospitals provide good and compassionate medical, nursing, and midwifery care, though women in less affluent neighborhoods are more likely to receive inferior, incomplete, and even disrespectful care. However, even in the best of circumstances, the continuity of support from a trusted mentor breaks down when women go into labor and enter the hospital. The worlds of medical care and social support do not intersect comfortably. Many women give birth surrounded by strangers and, perhaps, an equally frightened family member, and no matter how caring a health provider may be, we are still strangers to our patients.

The importance of childbirth resonates over time. It is linked to the circumstances of everyday life, to the constantly changing sweep of personal, family, and community history. In many cultures, the traditional practice of ongoing family and community support during pregnancy and lying-in held the family during this critical moment. In the United States, too many families are socially isolated and lack access to ongoing caring and support. Poverty, immigration, language barriers, and the growing mobility and fragmentation of families have made it increasingly difficult to provide the kind of family support that reflects this universal need. The increased diversity of the U.S. population, the increasing racial and ethnic disparities in health and early childhood status, and the breakdown of social and professional networks of support for parents and children have made clear the need to build a new system.

The doula role knits together support for birthing families. The community-based doula model develops the community's resources for ongoing, holistic networks of caring that extend over time. Our experience with implementing this model has shown us that we have a precious opportunity to influence outcomes for vulnerable families, if we link birthing support to their ongoing lives.

References

Daro, D. A., & Harding, K. A. (1999). Healthy Families America: Using research to enhance practice. *The Future of Children* , 9, 152–176.

Duggan, A. K., McFarlane, E. C., Windham, A. M., Rohde, C. A., Salkever, D. S., Fuddy, L., et al. (1999). Evaluation of Hawaii's Healthy Start program. *The Future of Children*, 9(1), 66–90.

Eng, E., Salmon, M. E., & Mullan, F. (1992). Community empowerment: The critical base for primary health care. *Family and Community Health*, 15, 1–12.

Fedder, D. O., Chang, R. J., Curry, S., & Nichols, G. (2003). The effectiveness of a community health worker outreach program on healthcare utilization of West Baltimore City Medicaid patients with diabetes, with or without hypertension. *Ethnicity and Disease, 13*, 22–27.

Hans, S., & Korfmacher, J. (2002). The professional development of paraprofessionals. *Zero to Three, 23*, 4–8.

Hill, M. N., Bone, L. R., & Butz, A. M. (1996). Enhancing the role of community health workers in research. *Image, 28*, 221–226.

Kistin, N., Abramson, R., & Dublin, P. (1994). Effect of peer counselors on breastfeeding initiation, exclusivity, and duration among low-income urban women. *Journal of Human Lactation, 10*, 11–15.

Koch, E., & Thompson, A. (1997). *Community health workers: A leadership brief on preventive health programs.* Washington, DC: Civic Health Institute at Codman Square Health Center, the Harrison Institute for Public Law at Georgetown University Law Center, & Center for Policy Initiatives.

Olds, D. L., Robinson, J., O'Brien, R., Luckey, D. W., Pettitt, L. M., Henderson, C. R., et al. (2002). Home visiting by paraprofessionals and by nurses: A randomized, controlled trial. *Pediatrics, 110*(3), 486–496.

Roman, L. A., Lindsay, J. K., Moore, J. S., & Shoemaker, A. L. (1999). Community health workers: Examining the helper therapy principle. *Public Health Nursing, 16*, 87–95.

Rosenthal, E. L. (1998). *A Summary of the National Community Health Advisor Study: Weaving the Future.* Tucson, AZ: University of Arizona.

Swider, S. M. (2002). Outcome effectiveness of community health workers: An integrative literature review. *Public Health Nursing, 19*, 11–20.

World Health Organization. (1978). Primary health care. Report of the International Conference on Primary Health Care, Alma-Ata. *Health for All Series, 1.* Geneva, Switzerland: Author.

Chapter 3

The Community-Based
Doula Model

T he community-based doula model is an emerging approach to
supporting new families, particularly in underserved communities. It is both
ancient—women have been supporting other women in childbirth since the human
community began—and innovative, with this support role rediscovered and rede-
fined. It is an intervention that fits into a variety of programs in diverse settings.
This chapter explores the community-based doula model and its essential components and describes community-based doula practice.

Chicago Health Connection's (CHC's) early work on community-based doulas
advanced significantly and developed into a model when, from 1996 through
2000, it was the lead agency in the Chicago Doula Project. The Chicago Doula
Project was a collaborative pilot project funded by the Irving B. Harris Foundation
and the Robert Wood Johnson Foundation to implement a doula program in
three community-based service agencies in Chicago. The partners in this effort
came from different disciplines
and approaches but shared
a commitment to developing
an intensive, extended,
relationship-based intervention
to support young families
through pregnancy, birth, and
the early postpartum period.

The 4-year pilot project
established the feasibility of
community-based doula work
embedded in programs

Photo by Liz Chilsen

29

providing long-term social support to families in underserved communities. The outcomes of the project reflected the outcomes reported in the literature: significantly lower rates of cesarean sections, lower rates of medical intervention during labor, and dramatically increased rates of breastfeeding (Altfeld, 2003). In addition, women who participated were more likely to receive recommended prenatal care, and younger mothers were less likely to have a rapid subsequent pregnancy. Anecdotal reports from the sites and observations of videotaped interactions also suggest a significant effect on mother–child attachment behaviors. From a variety of perspectives, the Chicago Doula Project was an exciting innovation. It engendered considerable interest in further research and in program replication. Chapter 4 discusses the project in greater detail.

The CHC Model

This model is exciting partly because it integrates a number of disciplines. It marries perspectives from maternal and child health, parent–infant attachment, infant mental health, and child development. It bridges the gap between health care and social services by defining an extended support role that begins in the home and community, continues with the birthing woman when she enters the hospital, and follows her back home with her baby in the early postpartum period. It is a unique collaboration that transcends traditional professional categories to strengthen families.

The doula intervention begins as early as possible during pregnancy, and the relationship continues through the early postpartum months. This sustained involvement allows doulas to accompany the family through the transformative experience of pregnancy, birth, and early parenting. With intensive training and reflective, supportive supervision, community-based doulas are expert guides to developing strong families.

The model is designed to serve families in diverse communities and to be able to be integrated into a variety of programs and settings. Community-based doula programs reside in vastly different agencies but all serve communities that have been self-defined as underserved. These programs have identified specific priority needs of birthing families that are not adequately addressed in their community, and they have selected the community-based doula model to serve those needs. Community-based doula programs serve their constituencies in somewhat different ways, but they all have in common a set of essential components.

Essential Components of CHC's Model

CHC's community-based doula model includes the following core components:

- Doulas are paid staff recruited and hired from the community being served.

- Participating families have extended involvement with doulas.

- Extensive training, ongoing reflective supervision, peer support, and administrative support are priority components of successful programs.

- Collaborative community partnerships are necessary to provide continuity of care to families.

- Communities define desired perinatal health and parent–infant relationship outcomes, and develop and refine the program to attain those outcomes.

From the same background. Doulas are laywomen, members of the community in which they work, so they understand the community and its culture. They have the same racial and socioeconomic background as the women they support. They are recognized and respected within their communities for their personal experience, their capacity to support and advocate for their neighbors, and their accurate basic knowledge of health promotion. They are hired and paid as formal service providers by agencies that serve the community. They nurture their clients, serve as role models, and act as liaisons to local health care systems. As one doula said, "Most of us live in the neighborhood where we work, so the teens listen to us."

Successful doulas share certain qualities: a commitment to helping women have satisfying births, a capacity to form strong trusting relationships, and an ability to listen and respond to a mother's needs. These women are committed to giving back to their community, which they do both formally as doulas and informally—on the street, in church, in the park—as community members. In their personal connections with mothers and families, doulas provide the human touch; nonjudgmental, supportive relationships that are personal as well as professional. The typical distance between client and service provider that is a part of many professional relationships is diminished in this intimate role. "They love us," said one teen mother about the doulas in her program. This can be a tricky path for providers and requires strong, supportive supervision and clear role definitions. But this intimacy may be responsible for the profound effect of community-based doula support.

Extended involvement with families. This is a long-term intervention, a family support program built on relationship-based caring over time. Our extended doula model fosters relationships from as early as possible in pregnancy well into the postpartum period. Both before and after childbirth, doulas offer direct support. They use this time to build a trusting relationship and to enhance the knowledge of the mother and family about proper prenatal care, with an early focus on the baby, early brain development, and the critical role parents play in shaping the emotional, social, and cognitive development of their children. The focus on building trusting relationships allows the nurturing of the new mother's needs and development as a parent and, ultimately, of a sensitive, responsive parenting style.

Training and support. CHC has developed an intensive training curriculum for community-based doulas. Our approach, based on Paulo Freire's popular education, is similar to that used to train community health workers (CHWs) worldwide. The format is personal and interactive and reinforces self-esteem and empowerment. Group discussions, role play, presentations by speakers, and in-depth curriculum materials are all used in the training program. This training approach is critical to the success of the program. We describe it in more detail in chapter 5.

Community-based doula work is relationship based on all levels. The model emphasizes nurturing the nurturers. If doulas are to develop nurturing relationships with families, they need to have experience of supportive nurturing relationships in the workplace (Bernstein, Campbell, & Akers, 2001). Supervision that is reflective makes relationships central to the work and focuses on strengths. It allows for thoughtful exchange around the work with families and the experience of the doula.

Collaborative community partnerships. CHC's approach to the community-based doula model relies on partnerships to promote better health. We believe that professionals must attend to the needs, perceptions, and strengths of communities to improve the health of underserved populations. CHC collaborates with community partners across the country to replicate the core model, developing partnerships among key stakeholders, including service professionals, local health and social service organizations, financial donors, community residents, and health care providers.

Optimizing outcomes. Our approach to defining program outcomes is both problem focused and asset based. Community-based doula work is particularly important in communities where families face considerable challenges, where poor maternal and child health and child development status reflect those difficult conditions. These communities are often labeled high risk, and birth outcomes and optimum school readiness are only two of the areas in which health and social disparities exist.

Effective programs are developed from a focus on desired program outcomes. One approach to this process is the use of a logic model, or "theory of change" (Diehl, 2002). Early in the process of program development, time is invested in defining what outcomes are priorities for the community and what key program activities or elements must be in place to achieve the outcomes. These outcomes may include a variety of priorities, from increased spacing of pregnancies in an adolescent parenting program to continuing recovery in an addiction treatment center. However, all community-based doula programs have in common a focus on promoting maternal and child health and fostering optimal parent–infant inter-action.

Community-Based Doula Practice

The essence of doula practice is in the supportive relationship. The community-based doula begins a relationship with the client as early as possible in the pregnancy. The doula makes home visits, provides prenatal education, accompanies the expectant mother to prenatal appointments, supports her during labor and birth, and provides support and education during the early postpartum period. In the context of a long-term relationship, the doula accomplishes goals through a variety of activities and in different venues.

During pregnancy. The months before birth are a critical time for the doula's work. This period allows the doula and her client to establish a relationship. It provides time for the doula to develop an understanding of the client's needs and concerns, to educate her about pregnancy and her growing fetus, and to develop a birth plan, which includes her preferences about options and procedures in labor. Learning about signs of labor and the physiology of birth helps the young mother feel more comfortable and less fearful. Prenatal education can be done

one-on-one during home visits, during clinic appointments, or in prenatal classes or groups.

Birth. For most women, childbirth is fraught with anticipation and apprehension. The unfamiliar environment of the hospital can be stressful and intimidating. However, for some women, such as low-income young women who do not speak English, this is likely to be an even greater journey into the unknown and a more frightening experience. The doula can act as a buffer, a nurturing presence, for a vulnerable young mother. In addition to informing clients about what to expect and what is occurring, the doula can communicate this information to family members and partners, who also may feel uncomfortable or intimidated in this alien environment.

The doula also serves as a bridge for communication between the client and her health care providers, encouraging her to be her own advocate. One way to accomplish this is to use the birth plan developed during prenatal visits to help the client communicate her preferences to caregivers.

Postpartum. The community-based doula continues her supportive role during the postpartum period, typically making home visits for at least 12 weeks. The frequency and duration of postpartum visits vary. Usually doulas make several visits during the first week, depending on the client's needs, and then gradually decrease the frequency. During this time, the doula acts as a role model for the new mother; educates her about her infant's needs, care, and normal development; and helps her learn how to be responsive to her baby.

By visiting the new mother often in the days after birth, the doula is able to provide vital support for the breastfeeding mother. Despite the desire or intent to breastfeed, many new mothers encounter difficulties that may quickly prove overwhelming without timely and skillful support and encouragement. A knowledgeable, trusted doula can be instrumental in a young mother's ability to breastfeed successfully.

The doula is also in a unique position to help the new mother process her birth experience. The doula is a participant at the birth, but she is a more objective presence, being neither family member nor health care provider. As someone with considerable experience with birth, she can help the mother make sense of her experience.

Community-based doulas have the opportunity to engage and nurture young parents through the particular emotional openness and receptiveness that occurs around pregnancy, birth, and early parenting. They are protectors of the rites of passage. Doulas have the honor of being present with families at some of the most significant moments in their lives—to witness, support, and reflect back to them their strength and growth. This significant presence gives doulas a unique opportunity to affect the lives of new parents in a particularly intimate way. Community-based doula support makes the best use of the experiences of pregnancy, birth, and early parenting to optimize the growth and development of parents and infants.

References

Altfeld, S. (2003). *The Chicago Doula Project Evaluation final report*. Chicago: The Ounce of Prevention Fund.

Bernstein, V. J. , Campbell, S., & Akers, A. (2001). Caring for the caregivers: Supporting the well-being of at-risk parents and children through supporting the well-being of programs that serve them. In J. N. Hughes, A. M. La Greca, & J. C. Close (Eds.), *Handbook of psychological services for children and adolescents* (pp. 107–132). New York: Oxford Press.

Diehl, D. (2002). *Issues in family support evaluation: Report from a meeting of national thought leaders*. Chicago: Family Support America.

Chapter 4

The Chicago Doula Project

This chapter is an exploration of the Chicago Doula Project, the 4-year pilot project that developed and tested the community-based doula intervention, which took root when Chicago Health Connection (CHC) had the good fortune to meet Irving Harris in 1995. Irving was a passionate advocate for the health and well-being of infants and families. As a businessman, he had built a fortune. As a citizen of the world, he set out to solve society's ills. He focused his philanthropy on programs that intervened in support of families at risk. He had provided funding in the 1980s for the initial birth doula research of Drs. John Kennell and Marshall Klaus.

Irving was intrigued by the potential he saw in the doula model and was looking for a way to implement it with families facing particular challenges. Through his efforts, we were brought together in a collaborative effort with three community-based agencies in Chicago that served pregnant and parenting teens—Marillac Social Center (called Marillac House by the local community), Christopher House, and Alivio Medical Center—and in July 1996, with local funding support from the Harris Foundation and the Robert Wood Johnson Foundation, the Chicago Doula Project was born. The Ounce of Prevention Fund coordinated the program evaluation.

The Chicago Doula Project trained and employed a cadre of laywomen as doulas to provide prenatal, intrapartum, and postpartum support to birthing teens enrolled in the three agencies. Besides providing direct service to an underserved, vulnerable population in Chicago, the project was designed to integrate a practice previously used with middle-income populations into the existing service provision in three different low-income urban settings.

With CHC as the lead agency, the community-based doula model was developed in these three disparate settings. In the 4-year pilot project (1996–2000), doulas provided support to almost 290 pregnant and parenting teens and their families.

This project caught the imagination of the communities involved and the interest of local and state policymakers. It was launched with the extraordinary personal and financial support of Irving Harris and matching funds from the Robert Wood Johnson Foundation's Local Initiatives Funding Partners Program. The collaborators thought that a program providing appropriate, culturally sensitive social support to enhance the strengths and resources of teens during pregnancy, birth, and early parenting would have a long-term effect on the health of mothers and children and the growing parent–child relationship. This model, in fact, has proven to be of sustained benefit to the local communities that developed it and, ultimately, to a much broader audience.

The Community-Based Partners

The collaborating community-based agencies reflected diverse experiences and approaches. One of the project's strengths was the integration of one model of perinatal support into three very different structures. Each of the three sites participated in the Parents Too Soon (PTS) program for pregnant and parenting teens. PTS programs originally were initiated and funded through a public–private partnership of Irving Harris and the Illinois Department of Children and Family Services in 1983 and continue to be sustained by the Ounce of Prevention Fund, which is the contractor and administrative agent for the PTS program. The program works with pregnant adolescents and young parents throughout Illinois to encourage healthy pregnancies and births, high school completion, delay of subsequent pregnancies, and responsive parenting. The Chicago Doula Project was centered in established PTS programs, so that it could benefit from ready access to the target population, an entree into communities with which PTS had

had long and well-developed relationships, and the immediate advantage of working with sites that were already funded and operating.

Chicago Health Connection

As the community-based lead agency, CHC brought to the table the experience we gained coordinating a well-established internationally recognized breastfeeding peer counselor training and support program. We had trained peer counselors throughout Chicago and had trained trainers of peer counselors nationwide. The popular education approach of that program emphasized reinforcement of self-esteem and empowerment, and training was interactive and participant-driven—a dynamic model of health education and community development, focusing on personal and social change. Over a period of 10 years, we had trained more than 450 mothers in low-income communities and thousands of professional and lay health workers who served them to promote breastfeeding, infant immunizations, and other maternal and child health strategies.

Marillac House

Marillac House is a settlement house under the direction of the Daughters of Charity, serving an indigent African American community covering two adjacent neighborhoods, East Garfield and Near West, where the teen birth rates in 1996 were 26.6% and 24.6% of all births, respectively. Almost half of the residents of these neighborhoods were below age 25, and almost 22,000 neighborhood children lived in poverty. The percentage of female-headed households was the sixth highest in the city. The homicide rate was nearly four times higher than citywide rates; safety was a critical issue, both for community residents and for agency staff. Marillac's program for adolescent girls, Project Hope, offers to this day a support system linked with social and health care services to teens whose lives are constrained by a cycle of pregnancy and poverty.

Christopher House

Christopher House is a community-based social service agency serving eight of Chicago's North Side neighborhoods, including Logan Square, a Latino community characterized by cultural and economic isolation, and Uptown, a multicultural neighborhood where nearly one third of all families live in poverty. Christopher House's teen parenting program, Partners in Progress, was already serving approximately 60 adolescents and their children and extended families, providing home visiting, peer support groups, onsite general equivalency diploma (GED)/literacy classes, and a program assisting teen mothers in their passage to self-sufficiency. The program served a diverse group of Latina, African American, White, Native American, Vietnamese, Thai, and Cambodian young women.

Alivio Medical Center

Alivio Medical Center is a community-based health care center serving four of the largest Latino neighborhoods in Chicago. This area is a densely populated, young, working poor, predominantly Mexican American community with multiple barriers to health care. A 1987 needs assessment revealed that 40% of respondents were without any medical insurance, with an additional 10% without coverage beyond hospitalization, and 25% without family coverage. Seventy-seven percent of interviewed households had children under 18, and one in four households reported pregnancies within the past 2 years.

Alivio offered comprehensive health care services on a sliding scale, including a midwifery program and home visitor program, with a bilingual, bicultural clinical staff. The agency was serving about 80 pregnant teens per year.

Project Activities

CHC convened a collaborative Doula Work Group to plan and direct the development of the pilot project. The first step was to conduct a doula training for lay health workers, who would then integrate birthing support into the paraprofessional home visitor support and nursing services currently provided to pregnant and parenting teens at PTS project sites.

We trained nine women as lay doulas during Year 1 and created a full-time doula position at each site. Training was provided to the hired doulas, as well as to site supervisors, other site-based staff, and community members interested in this support role. The doula trainees not hired were available to the agencies contractually for backup if the staff doulas were not available because of illness or vacation. The training experience served as a first step for community involvement and potential career development for some community women not yet in the workforce. We trained a second class in Year 2, to allow for dropout and turnover.

Our 10-year experience in training peer counselors had highlighted the importance of extensive training for lay health workers supporting women in a clinical or medical area of health care. Our lay health worker doula training involved 60–70 hours of preservice classroom time over 3 months, with subsequent monthly in-service training and discussion classes. The training used an interpersonal, participatory approach including role play, group discussion, and extensive practice. Participants observed at least three births. Course content included a range of perinatal topics, such as physiological changes during pregnancy and labor, communication and relaxation techniques, breastfeeding support, infant care, and infant development.

At the time, there was no published curriculum specifically developed for paraprofessional doulas from low-income communities and communities of color. Therefore, CHC developed a curriculum appropriate to the learning styles, literacy levels, and experience with formal education levels common among community-based doulas in training, a curriculum that included a focus on cultural competence and an interactive process. The curriculum has been a foundation of our model replication work across the country. Chapter 8 discusses CHC's replication of the community-based doula model in more detail.

The CHC Training Team—which included a certified doula/registered nurse, a health educator experienced in paraprofessional training, and CHC's peer counselor coordinator—provided additional training and ongoing technical assistance as needed to staff at participating sites, in partnership with the doula trainees. In addition, the lay doulas were offered the opportunity to achieve doula certification through Doulas of North America (DONA), thereby developing a community resource that would outlast the funded project.

The Extended Doula Model

CHC knew from our ongoing work with underserved communities that supporting a woman around childbirth is not enough if that support is not linked to her ongoing life—before and after the birth. We brought this knowledge to the Chicago Doula Project, developing a model that extended the doula role past the labor and delivery support documented by Klaus and Kennell (1997) into a long-term relationship from early pregnancy through the postpartum period.

From our previous mother-to-mother support work, we also knew that the community-based doula intervention that we were developing should be built on a long-term relationship, strength based, and personal. Therefore, the doulas met their clients during pregnancy, as early as possible. They had regular contact with the pregnant teens, both in home visits and center-based activities. The doulas accompanied the teens to prenatal visits with the

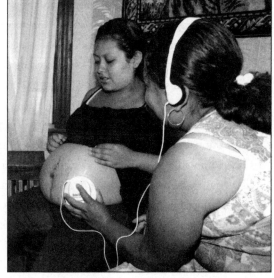

Photo by Liz Chilsen

doctor or midwife, encouraging them to ask questions and interpreting medical information in an individualized manner. Doulas supported the young women in developing a birthing plan, detailing their preferences for pain control, management of labor, support systems, and infant feeding. They presented prenatal education in a way that encouraged the teens to take an active role in their health, their health care, and the well-being of their babies. They nurtured these mothers-to-be with hugs, massage, caring words, and information. The doulas focused the mothers' attention on their relationships with their babies, on their hopes and dreams for their futures, and on setting and achieving life goals.

The doula was available to the teen when labor began, helping her determine whether she was actually in labor; making sure she contacted her care provider; knowing when and how she should go to the hospital; and supporting her through labor, delivery, and the first hours postpartum.

The doula met the teen at the hospital when it was time to go. She provided an ongoing supportive presence during the entire labor and delivery, focusing on both physical and emotional support as labor progressed. The doula was there at the mother's side as the baby was born, holding her hand, breathing with her, providing physical comfort and emotional support. The doula was there to latch the baby onto the breast in the delivery room. She returned the next day to witness the mother's transformation, help with breastfeeding, and exult over the baby. She continued support through the early weeks of parenting, helping both parents make sense of their new roles, the amazing capacities of the newborn, and the mechanics of infant care and feeding.

In the immediate postpartum period, the doula reviewed the events of labor and delivery, reassured the mother that her baby was normal and healthy, provided breastfeeding support, and facilitated attachment and infant care. During the first week postpartum, the doula had three to five contacts with the new mother. During the following 6 to 12 weeks, depending on the needs of the family and other services available, the doula was a resource to the new mother in coordination with the home visitor, during which time she helped to transition the home visitor into the primary support role for the duration of the teen's involvement in the program. The pace of this transition was decided collaboratively by the agency project staff and the participants.

Pilot Project Outcomes

Women who participated in the pilot project responded to this supportive caring, provided at just the right moment. They displayed an openness to learning, growth, and change. As had been documented in the research literature, teen mothers in the Chicago Doula Project had low cesarean-section rates, low rates of epidural analgesia, and high breastfeeding rates. One of the original pilot sites described how the project enhanced the services they were providing to young families:

> We're getting the girls in a lot earlier in their pregnancies than we used to, and they are now better prepared for labor and delivery and motherhood. And I think that the relationship with a person, the doula, who treats birth as special is meaningful to the participants. There is a stronger focus on the pregnancy and the birth now in our program…. They [the participants] definitely have more knowledge and understanding about baby's development, more aware of the importance of talking to the baby, eye contact, and breastfeeding. They're not grossed out by it [breastfeeding]. And they understand the importance of physical contact with the baby. And we're seeing a lot of girls…earlier in pregnancy when we often didn't see them until the baby was a couple of months old. (Maureen)

Outcomes of the 4-year pilot project were impressive (Altfeld, 2003). The Ounce of Prevention Fund collected data from teens receiving doula services through participating sites and compared them with data on pregnant and parenting teens who did not receive doula services. During 3.5 years of service provision, doulas provided support to almost 300 families; 259 women who gave birth to 267 babies were included in the research sample. Teen mothers with doula support had the following:

- Significantly lower cesarean-section rates (8.1% for doula-attended births compared with 14.5% for U.S. teens and 12.9% for Chicago teens),

- Significantly lower epidural rates (11.4% of vaginal births compared with a conservative estimate of 50% nationwide), and

- Significantly higher breastfeeding initiation rates (80.1% compared with 47.3% for U.S. teens and 42% for all Illinois women).

At one site, Marillac House, the breastfeeding initiation rate increased from almost no breastfeeding to 65% within the first year of the project and stayed at that level for the duration of the pilot project. At 6 weeks, 62.3% of all project participants were still breastfeeding, and 21% were still breastfeeding at 6 months.

Other broader outcomes were also impressive. Subsequent pregnancies were significantly delayed for younger mothers involved in the project. Mothers receiving doula support stayed longer in the program than mothers without a doula. Coded videotapes of mother–infant interaction showed significantly higher scores for the Nursing Child Assessment Satellite Training (NCAST) Feeding Scale (Sumner & Spietz, 1994) in the cognitive growth fostering subscale in sites where doula involvement began early in pregnancy, lasted until 12 weeks postpartum, and included group services, compared with less intensive programs. The pilot sites reported that participating teen moms were holding their babies more, talking to them more, and were more comfortable talking about their births, as in the following example:

> The moms are more sweet with their babies. They seem happier. They are talking about breastfeeding. They have a glow. They are more positive dur-

ing pregnancy, too. Also, they are telling their birth stories more and sharing their stories with each other. (Ana)

Another evaluation, a videotaping project conducted in 1999, compared the
mother–infant interaction of a small group of young mothers being served by
doulas with a demographically similar group of mothers not receiving doula support (Hans, 1999). Coding of the videotaped interactions using the Parent–Child
Observation Guide (Bernstein, Percanski, & Wechsler, 1996) showed that mothers in the doula group had better scores in maternal sensitivity and encouragement and guidance of the infant. These results were encouraging enough to
persuade the researchers to undertake a formal clinical research trial examining
the effect of the community-based doula intervention on mother and child outcomes and the parent–child relationship at the University of Chicago, which is
still in process.

The health outcomes of this intervention also translate into cost savings. In the
Ounce of Prevention evaluation of the Chicago Doula Project, cost savings
from the intervention totaled $7,439 per cesarean section averted, $1,000 per
epidural averted, and significant potential savings for reduced length of stay (Altfeld,
2003). For the 262 births in just over 3 years, the total cost savings for the reduced
cesarean sections and epidurals alone were estimated at over $180,000 (Altfeld,
2003). As many of the women receiving services were on Medicaid, these cost
savings directly affect the Medicaid program.

At the end of the 4-year pilot project, the outcomes indicated positive effects of
doula support on both immediate perinatal outcomes and potentially longer term
attachment and parenting issues. The partners in the original pilot project—both
the funding partners and the program partners—were passionately committed
to its success. In a period of great uncertainty about the future of health care funding, the funders and the partners saw this project as having great potential to be
of sustained benefit to the local communities that developed it and, ultimately,
to a much broader audience. The project's strong positive outcomes sparked intense
interest in replicating the community-based doula model. With generous sup-

port from the Harris Foundation and other national and local funders, CHC developed the Harris Doula Institute in July 2000 to partner with agencies around the country to integrate doula programs into their family support services. (See chapter 8.)

References

Altfeld, S. (2003). *The Chicago Doula Project Evaluation final report.* Chicago: The Ounce of Prevention Fund.

Bernstein, V. J., Percansky, C., & Wechsler, N. (1996). Strengthening families through strengthening relationships: The Ounce of Prevention Fund Developmental Training and Support Program. In M. C. Roberts, (Ed.), *Model programs in child and family mental health* (pp. 109–133). Mahwah, NJ: Lawrence Erlbaum.

Hans, S. L. (1999, January 7). *Doula intervention pilot videotaping project. Report to the Harris Foundation* (pp. 1–20). Chicago: University of Chicago, Department of Psychiatry.

Klaus, M., & Kennell, J. (1997). The doula: An essential ingredient of childbirth rediscovered. *Acta Paediatrica, 86,* 1034–1036.

Sumner, G., & Spietz, A. (Eds.). (1994). *NCAST caregiver/parent-child interaction feeding manual.* Seattle: NCAST Publications, University of Washington.

Chapter 5

Nurturing the Nurturers: Doula Recruitment, Education, and Support

"How you are is as important as what you do" (Pawl & St. John, 1998) is a central tenet of the infant–family field, and the community-based doula model perfectly reflects this truth. The model nurtures the development of consistent, trusting relationships. This, in fact, is one of the ways in which the doula intervention can profoundly affect the lives of parents and their children. Therefore, the success of the model depends on hiring doulas who possess qualities and develop skills that enable them to develop supportive relationships with parents. It is equally important that, once hired, doulas receive training, supervision, and support that nurtures them, and the development of doula programs must provide a structure for this. Doulas' support for the process of growth and change, which depends on a nurturing culture in the management of doula programs, is as important as the content of home visits or prenatal education.

This chapter focuses on how to recruit, educate, supervise, and support doulas within the community-based doula model.

Recruitment and Selection

Although most community-based doulas are from the community being served, sometimes they do live outside the local community. In either case, doulas must be able to identify with women living in the target community, and the women must be able to identify with them. In other words, the doulas must reflect the cultural and social realities of the community and come from similar backgrounds or experiences. They must understand the spoken and unspoken language of the community and share values, attitudes, and experiences with the women they will serve. They must be good advocates for themselves and for others, and they must know how to listen to and connect with others. Doulas must have family support to allow them to go out when needed in the middle of the night to meet a mother in labor. They must feel comfortable and know how to be safe making home visits in the neighborhoods and be committed to improving their communities. Above all, they must be emotionally available to build trusting, nurturing relationships with their clients.

For agencies that have not had extensive experience working with community-based health workers, recruitment of community-based doulas can be a challenge. It may be helpful to use the National Community Health Advisor Study (Rosenthal, 1998) results as a framework for defining the doula role and selecting doulas. Although the study identified core roles, skills, and qualities of community health advisors, we have found the results applicable to community-based doulas. For community-based doulas, as for community health advisors, the qualities and skills they bring to the work—who they are—are what is important for their success. These characteristics, as defined by Rosenthal (p. 6) are delineated in Table 5.1:

Table 5.1

Qualities of Community Health Advisors	
• Connected to the community (a community member or possessing shared experience with community members)	• Motivated and capable of self-directed work
	• Caring
	• Empathetic
• Strong and courageous (healthy self-esteem and the ability to remain calm in the face of harassment)	• Committed/dedicated
	• Respectful
	• Honest
• Friendly/outgoing/sociable	• Open/eager to grow/change/learn
	• Dependable/responsible/reliable
• Patient	• Compassionate
• Open-minded/nonjudgmental	• Flexible/adaptable

Rosenthal also describes the roles typically played by community health workers, listed in Table 5.2:

Table 5.2

Seven Community Health Advisor Core Roles

- Cultural mediation between communities and health and human services system
- Informal counseling and social support
- Providing culturally appropriate health education
- Advocating for individual and community needs
- Ensuring people get the services they need
- Building individual and community capacity
- Providing direct services

Finally, agencies should look for potential doulas who possess or have the capacity for the skills listed by Rosenthal (1998) in Table 5.3:

Table 5.3

Core Skills of Community Health Advisors

- Communication skills
- Interpersonal skills
- Knowledge base
- Service coordination skills
- Capacity-building skills
- Advocacy skills
- Teaching skills
- Organizational skills

Recruitment

Because community-based doulas may not have had work experience, and because their role requires qualities that differ from those required for traditional professional roles, agencies need to pay particular attention to recruitment. The recruitment process may easily take 2 to 3 months.

Recruit doulas by both informal and formal means. Craft a job announcement that clearly describes the demands and benefits of the position. Post job announcements at the recruiting agency, at other community agencies and health care settings, and in public places, such as laundromats, libraries, and schools. Send announcements to health and social service providers and other formal community leaders, such as ministers and aldermen, and to informal leaders, such as community organizers, outreach workers, and community volunteers. An open community meeting on the doula program (see chapter 8) is another good opportunity to recruit doulas.

Selection

As many doulas say, this work is more than a job—it is a mission. Finding the right person for the role is more complicated than filling other, more defined service staff positions. Doula applicants should be interviewed by a small team. Beyond the traditional interview questions, it is important to ask about the applicant's experience with birth and breastfeeding and to listen for any issues she may have around her own experience that might get in the way of her supporting other women. It is helpful to get a sense of why applicants are interested in this kind of work, the depth of their commitment, and what experience they have had working with other women in the community.

Look for accepting, nonjudgmental attitudes, flexible approaches to different situations and people, and respect for the capacities of infants and their families. Situational questions can be useful, such as, "What would you do if you visited a pregnant teen and her mother was drunk?"or "What would you do if you arrived at a client's home and no one was there for the third visit in a row?" Be clear about the demands of this work, and ask specific questions about applicants' capacity and support for the job, such as whether they would be able to go out in the middle of the night to meet a woman at the hospital.

Finally, it is possible, and sometimes preferable, to recruit participants for doula training and subsequently hire one or more of the most outstanding trainees into available positions. The training itself can be an excellent screening tool. The interactive process of community-based training reveals the participants' strengths and weaknesses, and the 70–80 hours of class provide much more opportunity for observation and assessment than interviews. Women who successfully complete the training but are not hired for a full-time position can provide backup doula services on a part-time or occasional basis.

Ultimately, the doula intervention succeeds or fails based on the quality of the doulas. It is worth spending as much time as is needed to make a good decision. Becoming a doula is personally and professionally transforming. Women who have not been recognized for their experience and capacities become honored in this role. "It's like being a legend in my own community," said one doula. Behnke (Behnke & Hans, 2002) described the transition of a small group of women from doula training through the beginning of doula practice and concluded that the women who successfully embraced this new identity were changed in fundamental ways, particularly emotionally:

> They said that doula training changed their thinking, enabled them to take risks, made them feel understood and heard, and nurtured them…. The trainees revealed increased self-pride, excitement and optimism about their future, and enthusiasm for this new profession. (Behnke & Hans, 2002, p. 12)

Training

The educational approach we use in doula training is central to the success of Chicago Health Connection's (CHC's) community-based doula model. Our training philosophy rests on an assumption that gaining knowledge through an active, personal, and analytical process is potentially life-changing, and our approach to training is rooted in theories of learning as well as our 20 years of listening to the communities with whom we have partnered.

Our training approach emphasizes reinforcing participant self-esteem and sense of competence. Interactive learning and reflective evaluation enhance each session's content. Training methods include group discussion, role-play, journaling, and the use of multiple speakers, and the training curriculum integrates relevant, current clinical experiences. Doulas of North America (DONA) recognizes CHC's community-based doula training as fulfilling a requirement toward DONA certification.

CHC also trains community-based doulas for local replication programs in Illinois and surrounding areas. For national doula replication sites, we use a train-the-trainer model to teach local teams of trainers how to provide direct training to community based doulas. Our training teams include both clinically based registered nurses and midwife trainers and community-based trainers whose knowledge and experience lie in working with the community. Both areas of expertise are equally essential to the success of the training.

Theories of Learning

We base our instructional approach to doula training on several theories of learning. We have been influenced especially by Paulo Freire's educational philosophy (Freire, 1970), which was a source of inspiration for the Latin American popular education movement, and by applications of Freirean approaches developed as "Training for Transformation" (Hope, Timmel, & Hodzi, 1984). We have also been influenced by the techniques of imaginal education, a learning approach developed by the Institute of Cultural Affairs (Packard, 2000; Seagren, 1988; Spencer, 1989). In addition, we have drawn from those who have developed approaches to transformative learning (Taylor, Marienau, & Fidler, 2000).

Popular education. Popular education, sometimes called empowerment education, is a dynamic, effective, and revolutionary model that has been applied to health education and community development. This approach focuses on personal and collective change. Paolo Freire, a Brazilian educator, wrote that adults learn what is necessary to help them make change in their own lives and in their community. The trainer's role is to facilitate a discovery process that supports action and to support participants in discovering what they know, integrating new information, and setting their own development goals and agenda.

The principles of popular education emphasize listening and responding to the community's concerns. To be successful in harnessing this powerful resource, CHC training encourages doula trainees to connect the personal with the theoretical and to think critically about the problems, resources, and potentials in their midst. Through training, participants develop the potential to reflect on a critical analysis of their personal experiences and to begin to move toward action in their own lives and in their communities. This commitment to personal and social transformation characterizes the varied applications of popular education, including those used in literacy training, community organizing, civic participation, and health promotion.

Imaginal education. Imaginal education is based on the understanding that

Courtesy University of Chicago

people think in images, and that these images govern their behavior. Images create mindsets. If we believe that true learning occurs as we change from one mindset to another, training is most effective in catalyzing new behavior when the training takes into account the limiting mindset, or image, that is governing the ineffective behavior of participants. Through the imaginal education process, the activities and information experienced by learners challenge the old image and invite the formation of a new image or mindset, informed by new information and new experience.

To incorporate imaginal education and popular education in the CHC approach, we worked with the Institute of Cultural Affairs International (ICAI), drawing from their experience in community development across the world. ICAI consultants helped us organize our evolving curricula into a structure that captured the interactive process of our trainings and incorporated community themes that had emerged over the years.

Transformative learning. Transformative learning is a related approach to learning developed in the field of adult education. Malcolm Knowles popularized the concept of andagogy, or adult learning theory (Knowles, 1970). This approach is based on a definition of adult learning as self-directed, problem-based, and practical. It stresses respect for the life experiences of adult learners. Learning is seen as an active process within the learner, one that involves the whole person. To be effective, the learning must be cooperative and collaborative (Brillinger, 1990). Jack Mezirow (1978) defined this adult learning process as transformative learning, the process of making sense of one's experience. As with Freire's approach, transformative learning

Photo by Rachel Abramson

involves reformulating the meaning of experience. It is based on critical reflection and leads the learner to act on her new understandings (Mezirow, 1991).

All of these themes, which involve learning for the purpose of change, have been incorporated into CHC's community-based doula training and are reflected in the work of the doulas.

Training Curriculum

CHC's 20-session doula curriculum includes topics that are essential for preparing doulas to work with women in a community health setting, including, but not limited to, the following:

- Communication techniques;

- Attitudes, beliefs, and values;

- Emotional and physical labor support techniques;

- Obstetrical routines, interventions, and alternatives;

- Birth as a life event;

- Infant capacities;

- Breastfeeding; and

- The context of doula work.

Trainees are also required to complete a range of clinical experiences that include clinical observations, prenatal childbirth preparation classes, birth observations, and a mentored birth.

Because every community is different and every program has its own assets and needs, our 20-session training curriculum is just the beginning of ongoing doula training, which is tailored to each program setting. Additional preservice training or continuing education may be required to prepare doulas for particular community issues or when new components are added to a program. Additional training might include content such as substance abuse and recovery, breastfeeding support, or home visiting principles. Some agencies incorporate other curricula into their programs, such as Healthy Families, STEEP, Community-Based Family Administered Neonatal Activities, or other materials that also help promote attachment.

CHC keeps the content of our training at a level appropriate for the layperson. Doula training should be seen as a basic-level course; it is not intended to train expert-level practitioners. The doula training experience is designed to guide participants into their new roles by connecting their personal experiences with the content of the training in the context of a supportive, introspective group process. The intent is to develop paraprofessional practitioners who are able to use their self-awareness, mastery of the basic knowledge base, and community leadership to support families in their own communities.

In-Service Training

Preservice training and clinical observations are only the beginning of the doula's learning. There should be a smooth, natural transition from the safety of classroom time to the gradual development of a deeper competence through experience and practice. As one doula explains:

> You have to step back and listen and see where the participants are coming from. It takes three or four or five births to know when to listen, when to put hands on, when not to. Because everybody doesn't want to be touched. And it takes a while to learn that…it's a learning process. (Sandra)

This experience seems to be profound for the trainers as well as for participants. It takes a while to learn how to facilitate learning and change, rather than simply to transfer information:

> When I think about how green I was at the first class and how I grew as a trainer, but more importantly, as a human being, I feel proud to have been

a part of the doula training. The most important and profound thing for me, as a trainer, was how much I learned from the participants and from their life experience and wisdom. It was very humbling to be part of a process that recognized that we all learn from each other, all the time, and that no one has a monopoly on knowledge. The more time I spend in the world the more I realize how rare and how special that is. The beautiful thing about the doula training is that a culture of respect and a safe place to share thoughts and emotions was created. It was empowering for some of the women trained as doulas, certainly, but it was also empowering for the trainers. I think it was all the more powerful because of the subject matter; the issues surrounding pregnancy and birth which are, in and of themselves, profoundly life-changing. (Judy)

The experience of training—of emotional growth and change—is not always easy or smooth. Change can be challenging, humbling, and even painful. It can also be exhilarating and, at times, transforming. It involves a personal recognition that the individual has the ability to be successful in the new role. In this case, there seems to be an awareness that the doula's own life experiences and personal strengths, combined with her growing knowledge and ongoing commitment to helping others, give her the power to support birthing families. This process parallels the growth of the doula's clients, women who are in a period of great challenge and life change. These new mothers also must learn that they have the power to nurture their new babies. Just as the training structures this process for the doula, the doula program intervention does the same for the new mothers. Both components require an investment of time and emotional support.

Reflective Supervision

Community-based doula work is relationship-based on all levels. The model emphasizes nurturing the nurturer. Responsive, nurturing relationships between doula and mother are enhanced by ongoing nurturing, respectful supervision for the doula.

A doula's direct supervisor schedules weekly supervision sessions that allow for reflection on the daily work, a focus on what is going well, and support with what is stressful (Bernstein, Campbell, & Akers, 2001). Supervision that is reflective makes relationships central to the work and identifies and nurtures strengths. Jeree Pawl (1994/1995) described reflective supervision as follows:

> Supervision exists to provide a respectful, understanding and thoughtful atmosphere where exchanges of information, thoughts and feelings about the things that arise around one's work can occur. The focus is on the families involved and on the experience of the supervisee. (p. 24)

Family support is personal work, and support around birth is particularly intimate. A doula's exposure to the emotional challenges of her clients' pregnancy, birth, and parenting can often bring up the emotional challenges of her own experiences. The emotional intensity of this personal work can overwhelm the doula's efforts on behalf of the women she serves. Reflective supervision acknowledges and accepts the personal nature of the work. Bernstein and his colleagues (2001) described it as follows:

> The nurturing role means to facilitate understanding, recognize strengths and encourage learning, but not to dictate. When the person being nurtured recognizes what is working and what his or her strengths are, the person begins to build on them. This is the natural course of growth and development. Acceptance, the foundation of nurturing, lies in the belief and in the trust that when a person understands and learns, that person will choose to do what is best (p. 127).

Reflective supervision is modeled on this nurturing role. This should be true as well for all the relationships in the doula program constellation:

> The trust and bonding we develop with our young participants is crucial to the success of the program. The doula nurtures the mother, and the supervisor nurtures the doula. The relationships are based on trust. This takes time, patience, love, and energy. The focus on every level is attachment: mother to baby, doula to participant, and supervisor to the doula. (Bonnie)

Other Supports

Because the doula is a lay person functioning in a medical setting, doulas need 24-hour access to a clinical medical or nursing expert for ongoing or emergency information and support. The clinical support provider is not a second supervisor but works closely with the direct, or line, supervisor to support appropriate practice, clear role boundaries, and ongoing professional development. Through 24-hour phone access, phone debriefing after births, and monthly case conferences, the clinical support provider offers ongoing continuing education, facilitates exploration and understanding of more complicated clinical issues, shares information that doulas need to help clients understand their treatment, and monitors doula roles and practice.

A foundation of a successful community-based doula program is the creation of an ongoing culture and community of doula growth and peer support. A monthly continuing education/networking group gives doulas an opportunity to continue to grow professionally and to get social support from their "sister" doulas. Loretha says:

> When you go on a birth and it's traumatic, you need to tell the story. You can't keep it inside; it'll eat away at you. So my thing was I didn't know anyone else to talk to but my children. I kept trying to tell them. And they were saying, "Mommy, you have to keep saying that? Okay, it was bloody. She was split open like a chicken. How many ways can you describe it?" So, when I came to class [doula training], I kept telling them, "It's doula language. Nobody else knows this." So that's where I did get my comfort—coming back to [doula] class.

Annual retreats allow time for reflecting on the work and reenergizing, and attendance at national meetings like the annual DONA conference keeps doulas motivated and informed about up-to-date innovations in the field. Continuing education and support are often seen as frills in family support programs, but they are investments well worth the time and money. Doula work is intense, and community-based doula training is a long and, thus, expensive commitment.

Doula burnout with resulting staff turnover is both costly to the program and to the families the program serves. Ultimately, the well-being of mothers and babies depends on ongoing support of the doulas that nurture them.

References

Behnke, E. F., & Hans, S. L. (2002). Becoming a doula. *Zero to Three, 23*, 9–13.

Bernstein, V. J. , Campbell, S., & Akers, A. (2001). Caring for the caregivers: Supporting the well-being of at-risk parents and children through supporting the well-being of programs that serve them. In J. N. Hughes, A. M. La Greca, & J. C. Close (Eds.), *Handbook of psychological services for children and adolescents.* New York: Oxford Press.

Brillinger, M.F. (1990). Helping adults learn. *Journal of Human Lactation, 6*, 171–175.

Freire, P. (1970). *Pedagogy of the oppressed.* New York: Seabury Press.

Hope, A., Timmel, S., & Hodzi, C. (1984). *Training for transformation: A handbook for community workers.* Gweru, Zimbabwe: Mambo Press.

Knowles, M. S. (1970). *The modern practice of adult education: Andragogy versus pedagogy.* Englewood Cliffs, NJ: Prentice Hall/Cambridge.

Mezirow, J. (1978). Perspective transformation. *Adult Education, 28*, 100–110.

Mezirow, J. (1991). *Transformative dimensions of adult learning.* San Francisco: Jossey-Bass.

Packard, K. E. (2000). The kaleidoscope teaching and learning strategy. In K. Taylor, C. Marienau, & M. Fidler (Eds.), *Developing adult learners* (pp. 114–119) San Francisco: Jossey-Bass.

Pawl, J. H. (December 1994/January 1995). On supervision. In : Eggbeer, & E. Fenichel, (Eds.), Educating and supporting the infant-family workforce: Models, methods and materials. *Zero to Three, 15*(3), 21–29.

Pawl, J. H., & St. John, M. (1998). *How you are is as important as what you do.* Washington, DC: ZERO TO THREE.

Rosenthal, E. L. (1998). *A summary of the National Community Health Advisor Study: Weaving the future.* Tucson: University of Arizona.

Seagren, R. (1988). Imaginal education. *In Context, 18*, 48–51.

Spencer, L. J. (1989). *Winning through participation.* Dubuque, IA: Kendall/Hunt.

Taylor, K., Marienau, C., & Fidler, M. (2000). *Developing adult learners.* San Francisco: Jossey-Bass.

Chapter 6

The Doula's Experience of the Work

T he complexity and the heart of the doula experience are best described by those who live it. This chapter explores community-based doulas' perspectives on their work. Their stories and reflections describe the essential principles that guide doulas in their interactions with young pregnant and parenting clients. Doulas discuss the scope of their practice—how they work with clients and develop a relationship over an extended period from pregnancy through childbirth and the postpartum period. Particularly meaningful are the doulas' perceptions of their effect on their clients. The experience of the clients is explored more fully in the following chapter. Finally, doulas examine the many challenges they experience and the rewards this work offers.

Guiding Principles

Doulas are guided in their work by a number of fundamental principles:

- Building a trusting relationship,

- Fostering the mother–baby relationship,

- Optimizing perinatal outcomes,

- Involving partners and family members to strengthen new families,

- Catalyzing growth and change, and

- Nurturing mothers to nurture babies.

Building a Trusting Relationship

The very essence of the doula's work is building a trusting relationship with her client. The community-based doula's effectiveness is due in large part to her client's ability to identify with her and, ultimately, to trust her. By sharing a similar background, the doula can understand the challenges her clients face. Loretha explains:

> If you've never been in need and had a person come to your rescue, you don't know how to pass that feeling along in a truthful way. You don't know deep down in your heart how that person is feeling unless you have walked that same path. We serve as role models. We are able to identify with some of the issues the teens are going through, because most of us were teen moms. Living in the communities helps us understand the problems and pressure the participants are faced with on a daily basis. We are not scared to go into the neighborhoods because they are our homes.

This close identification goes both ways. Wandy says:

> Many of us have experienced trauma in our own lives, and most of us were teen moms. We have common ground. We have suffered like the ones we are serving. When we're in the situations with teen moms, we hear ourselves a lot.

The doulas also convey a deep caring for their young mothers:

> I treat each client as if she was a sister or a close friend. That kind of intimacy is what makes the mother–doula relationship work. (Hao)

The caring, generosity, and love that the doulas convey often enable the vulnerable young women who are their clients to develop trust and allow the doulas to help them. Doulas share their own stories selectively, both as a way of connecting with clients and as a means of educating them. One doula whose baby had been delivered by cesarean section described how she shared her personal story with her clients and allowed them to see her scar.

For some teen clients whose mothers are unavailable, doulas can function as surrogate mothers. The doulas' personal experiences with birth, breastfeeding, and mothering provide the context. They are considered knowledgeable and authoritative—and are trusted sources of information and advice in large part because they are insiders. The clients know that the doulas are speaking from their own experiences, rather than from a medical perspective, and from their hearts, motivated by a desire for what's best for the mothers and babies.

Fostering the Mother–Baby Relationship

A primary goal of the community-based doula is building the mother–baby relationship by creating a focus on the baby. In this regard, her scope is far broader than that of the private practice doula. The doula accomplishes this work during prenatal classes, home visits, and parenting groups, using a variety of approaches.

One tool widely used by community-based doulas is the Community-Based FANA (Family-Administered Neonatal Activities; Cardone, Gilkerson, & Wechsler, in press). The Community-Based FANA is a set of prenatal and postpartum activities that connect parents with the presence and developing capacities of their baby. It is based on research that has shown that parents are more likely to attach to their newborns when they focus on and attach to the fetus, and that strong parent–infant attachment results from responsive and engaged interaction. Doulas learn how to promote the mother's recognition of her developing fetus, explore the mother's perception of her fetus, and promote attachment to her fetus and then to her newborn. As one doula describes it:

> It's the FANA we do during pregnancy and afterwards. It's "tell me about your baby, what is the baby telling us today?" It's putting words in the baby's mouth. The mom can think, "Oh, I hadn't thought about that." The baby is more real to them. They're able to see the baby as an individual better. Having the mom do the [FANA] activities—she's feeling in charge, empowered. That empowerment is such a positive thing. (Bonnie)

By nurturing, supporting, and educating the expectant and new mother, the doula enhances maternal responsiveness and positive interaction with her infant, thus promoting secure attachment. A creative strategy used by some doulas during prenatal classes to promote the teens' attachment to their unborn infants is to invite them to write love letters to their babies, such as the following:

I love my baby.

I love my baby when I feel it kicking.

I love you when you move all through the night.

I love you when I be talking to you.

I love you for doing so good when I am doing bad.

I love you because you are my body and you are all I have.

I care about you even if your daddy don't.

I know sometime you may feel like I don't care.

But I do.

Optimizing Perinatal Outcomes

During the prenatal period, the doula influences her client to engage in healthy behaviors, including good nutrition, obtaining regular prenatal care, and seeking medical attention if she experiences danger signs. During doula training, the doulas learn about these warning signs and are able to educate clients and family members to watch for them. In this way, doulas promote awareness of signs of complications, such as preeclampsia and preterm labor, so that early intervention can help prevent premature births and the low birth weights associated with them. Many of these young mothers are at increased risk of poor obstetrical outcomes. The improved perinatal outcomes associated with the continuous support provided by doulas at birth are widely recognized and have been addressed in chapter 1.

Involving Partners and Family Members

An important goal of a doula's work is to include her client's partner and family members. She recognizes that her time with the client is limited and that the role of the teen's mother—the grandmother—and other family members is powerful and enduring. Therefore, when the grandmother can be brought in as an ally of the doula, her chances of being trusted and of being called for the birth are greatly enhanced.

In addition to focusing on strengthening the mother–infant relationship, the doula strengthens the new family by involving the baby's father. She does this by facilitating communication between the young mother and her partner and by encouraging his participation at the birth and his subsequent involvement with both mother and infant. "When you involve the dads more, they tend to stick around." (Loretha)

Rosalba describes her approach to involving partners in her classes:

> Invite them to your prenatal class and talk to them about how they feel about the birth, what's going to happen. What is their role; what do they plan to do? Do some role-playing work as a couple. Role-play the whole birth scenario. Review the setting at the hospital, so when they're at the hospital they'll feel comfortable. They already know me so dads will look at me. The dad asks what should I do next? Should I massage her? I say, "Ask her. Go towards her; ask her if she feels like being touched." Suggesting to them, and they feel, okay, I can do this. They will ask me, "Is she doing ok?" and I say "Why don't you ask her?" So they would get some cues from me and then go ahead and do it.

One doula tells a story of what she describes as an "extreme measure" to involve a partner at birth:

> The relationship between the teen and her boyfriend wasn't so good. She wanted him to be a part of the birth. She thought that by including him

that they would bond and he would respect her as the mother of his child.

The doula described a long labor at which the partner was present but remained apart from the client. He alternated between watching TV and trying to sleep:

> And I felt that she really wanted him to help her, but she was this type of person who really didn't know how to express it. I was with her constantly, holding her hand, and then he started snoring, and it wasn't just a small snore. And I thought, "Oh no, I can't let this happen." I thought he's missing out a lot. This is the time he can bond with her and get that closeness that they've been having trouble with. So, I took extreme measures. I had some M&Ms for myself 'cause I needed to stay awake. And I was reflecting on this, and I thought well maybe if I throw some M&Ms, he'll get up.

He woke up with a start, just as the girl began struggling to cope with another strong contraction. Responding to his startled expression, the doula said, "You need to get over here; she needs you."

> And she was in transition, so this was a perfect opportunity. And he picked himself up and went to her right away. And from then on he just stayed with her. So I just moved back. I thought, "If I don't do this, it's not going to work." So, it was perfect timing; he just took my shoes from there. He really focused on her and was encouraging her. I thought that was what she wanted. I noticed signs of relief. At first he didn't want to see the baby be born, but all of a sudden, he got curious, and he wanted to see. It was really nice, but it just took two of those M&Ms....

Later, some days after the birth, the father told the doula that he was really happy that he was involved—"At first I didn't feel like I was a part of it. I didn't feel connected." The new mother said that after the birth the ties were getting stronger—he valued her more as a woman. He saw how much she suffered through the birth. He was being a good father, getting up with the baby.

Some weeks later, the doula's supervisor noted the striking change in this father. She asked, "What did you do? Before we couldn't even get him to be a part of it. Before, he would just stay out in the waiting room." As a result of an unusual and creative solution, this doula was able to effect a striking change in one father's level of involvement with the teen

Photo by Liz Chilsen

mother and infant. This is an example of the way doulas can facilitate change within the family. As Cicero noted long ago, "The beginnings of all things are small."

Catalyzing Change

In the context of a long-term trusting relationship, the doula has the opportunity during the pregnancy and postpartum period to help the young mother develop her own potential:

> I give her back the trust she has within herself. Their minds and bodies are so powerful. They have that strength within. It's not in the books, the doctors, or me. It's in them…but it's being pushed away by fear, by society, by being put down. (Sandra)

The opportunity to master the challenging transitions of pregnancy, childbirth, and early parenting can be an important developmental step for young women. The doula supports the new mother's capacity to make decisions and to act on her choices:

> You don't realize when you're empowering these young girls until it's happening right there — right at the birthing bed when they say, "Bina, should I get the epidural?" I'm not supposed to give my opinion. And how it works

> ... is, "You're doing so great. You are so strong." ... And this empowers a
> woman to say, "Yeah, I'm going to try to make it without the epidural."

> I just had an experience, and it was beautiful. She was so empowered that
> as ... she was still being sutured ... she was on the phone calling her
> friends and family, "I had my baby, and I did not use the epidural." It was
> so great how she felt empowered, how strong she felt that she didn't have
> to use the epidural. And I thought, "Oh, this is empowerment...give them
> the power to feel their strength." (Bina)

Another way that doulas help clients realize their potential is in the area of breastfeeding. A woman's perception of her ability to breastfeed successfully is essential to making the decision to initiate breastfeeding. If a woman does not think she can be successful, then she is unlikely even to try. This lack of confidence is one of many formidable barriers to breastfeeding. The doula can be especially effective in enhancing the self-efficacy of her pregnant teen and new mother clients.

By respecting the young mother and fostering her capacity to make her own decisions, rather than attempting to solve her problems for her, the doula can help women transform their lives for the better. Loretha says:

> A lot of them, it's like their words have been taken away. Things happen to
> them, and they become passive. They don't see any way out. I figure if we
> don't teach them, then they're not going to be able to teach their children.

Nurturing Mothers, Nurturing Babies

Klaus, Kennell and Klaus (2002) described the essential concept of mothering the mother. Being the recipient of the doula's nurturing care enables the mother to learn how to nurture her new infant. This parallel process characterizes the entire model.

Juana, a program director, describes how the doula can promote attachment between the young mother and her baby by the focus on the pregnant teen. She explains that the doctor's focus is on the well-being of the fetus. "With the doula's attention to the teen, she feels acknowledged and not just a vessel for the baby. She becomes more conscious of her value as the mother." Juana says that the nurses have noticed a change. In the past, nurses would report teen mothers in labor saying, "Get that thing out of me." Now nurses have commented that teens laboring with the support of a doula no longer speak about their babies this way.

Unlike many in the health care professions and in society at large, where disapproval of teen pregnancy is openly expressed, doulas accept the reality of the teens' pregnancies. Many of them were teen mothers themselves. They encourage the young mothers to be proud of themselves and their babies and to be the best mothers they can.

Michele, a program coordinator, describes an approach her program uses:

> As part of our doula/family facilitator program, we consider baby showers to be an essential component of our work. In explaining this to potential program funders, we are often met with surprise that we would "reinforce" childbearing by these women, who are most often young, single, and poor, and often having their second or third child. We explain that by celebrating each birth and baby as unique and special, the mother's attachment to this baby is facilitated and strengthened, which makes it less likely that she will become pregnant again right away.... The vast majority of our mothers space their subsequent pregnancies by at least 2 years, which we feel is an important predictor of healthy attachments.

Aspects of Doula Work

Doula work is diverse, but there are aspects common to many programs, including home visiting, prenatal breastfeeding support, peer group education, belly casting, and, of course, birthing support.

Home Visiting

Home visiting is an essential component of doula programs. Much of a doula's work in building a relationship with her client and the family, in providing information and support, occurs during these visits. As one doula/doula supervisor explains:

> It is important to be there for the visits, to be consistent, to be very clear, very open to what you can do and what you cannot do. You have to do what the client wants you to do, so that she develops that trust that "the doula is really there for me; she wants to get along with the family" that really helps build a relationship. And it's really important to listen to the girls. She not only listens but she asks those questions … so she's able to determine the girl's learning style early, and all of a sudden the girl is thinking, "This woman really wants to teach me stuff." … I think that kind of thing is really important in developing that relationship. (Bonnie)

The ability to go where the client lives gives a perspective on her life that can't be achieved in a center-based encounter:

> The first three visits I attended with this girl, she just said "yes" and "no." Those were the only answers she would give me even though I asked open-ended questions. She would look around to see if anyone was there or answer in a whisper. Then I knew something was going on. So I suggested we meet at the park. And her mom heard and said, "Oh, no, you can't go to the park. It's very dangerous; last week someone died of a gunshot wound there." It occurred to me that I had a van with a TV and VCR. And their VCR wasn't tracking too well. That's when I got creative; that's when my light bulb flickered. I told the mom that I could park my van right out in front. Once we started having visits in my van she was more willing to tell me what was going on in the home. She was more willing to express herself. The man her mom was living with was an alcoholic and violent towards her mother. She opened up a whole lot. (Wandy)

Some doulas work in agencies in which home visiting services already exist, and the doula program is another component of the agencies' services. Some doulas have already worked in the role of family support worker. For others, this may be their first experience with home visiting, and these doulas require considerable preparation and support to become comfortable in this role. Some visit clients in a small geographic area. Others may have to travel considerable distances, sometimes using public transportation, to reach their clients' homes.

Regardless of their personal experience, however, there are certain challenges that doulas are likely to face that are nearly universal. The primary one is access. Doulas tell stories of teens not being home or sometimes not answering the door even when they are, of hostile family members unwilling to allow the doula to enter the home, of clients with no phone, and so forth. Doulas also talk about lack of privacy during home visits in crowded or noisy studio apartments, of their discomfort visiting homes that are unclean or have roaches, of some clients with unstable living situations who move often or who are homeless, of dangerous neighborhoods where they are reluctant to travel alone, and of having to make arrangements to meet clients at neutral locations such as McDonalds. The intensity of this work is not confined to labor and delivery.

Prenatal Breastfeeding Support

Community-based doulas have proven highly effective in influencing young mothers to breastfeed. The health benefits of breastfeeding for both infant and mother are widely recognized. However, it is the potential for a positive effect on the mother's perception of the maternal role and her relationship with her infant that is of particular significance.

Many doulas explain that breastfeeding is not likely to be addressed during prenatal clinic appointments. Some of this may be due to time constraints. However, health care providers often hold biases or assumptions that lead them to believe that teens are unlikely to breastfeed their babies. Doulas speak about the importance of talking about breastfeeding prenatally and of the young mothers "seeing how it's done."

Doulas approach breastfeeding promotion in a variety of ways. The doulas' influence is based in part on the clients' awareness of how much the doulas care about them. Within the strength of this trusting relationship, the women believe in the advice that the doulas give. One doula describes her approach to clients:

> I have very strong views in terms of breastfeeding. I believe every woman should try. I say up front that this is a personal belief, that I'm biased. I feel if I'm up front, then there's no deception. I ask every woman to give me 1 week. If you run into trouble, give me 2 weeks. If that's too much to commit to, just give me 1 day. I may seem pushy, but I respect you if you say no. This is me; you can be you. As a person who breastfed eight children, I don't coerce. They may have a bottle-feeding family or may have a boyfriend who says "gross." I don't know their past. (Tracy)

Tracy's approach exemplifies the balance between being a passionate advocate for a healthy choice while maintaining respect for a mother's right to make her own decisions.

Peer Group Education

When the doula has an opportunity to work with clients in group prenatal and parenting classes, her influence is augmented by that of the peer group. The doula may be most effective when this relationship is embedded in a broader network of social support. At times, the doula can serve as a catalyst. For example, this appeared to be true in the area of increasing breastfeeding initiation at one social service agency serving clients on Chicago's West Side. The doulas working with the teens had breastfed their own children and encouraged the teens. Also—although the doulas provided the initial energy and impetus to promote breast-feeding—their enthusiasm generated interest in breastfeeding promotion among others at the agency, including home visitors. Once breastfeeding teens began appearing at parenting groups and were invited to talk to prenatal classes, the teens started to influence each other, resulting in what one doula describes as a "chain reaction." This change in the culture surrounding infant feeding method was sustained by a synergy between the doulas, the home visitors, and peers.

Many doulas and supervisors have spoken about the powerful effect of bringing the young women together. According to Bonnie:

> Things happen in group. It makes a big difference; it sets the girls up to stay in the program. They share a magic moment of pregnancy and birth. If they stay in a parenting group they've already built that trust, it's beautiful to see. They come in as perfect strangers.

Juana, a program director, describes the effect of having doulas provide prenatal classes:

> When the doula service was first offered, it was very hard to recruit clients; only 35% of eligible participants accepted the offer of a doula. They were reluctant to allow a doula to be present at birth partly because they didn't know her and didn't want her to see their body. However, they were eager to take prenatal classes, to learn about fetal development, nutrition, labor, bonding, and other topics. In the course of offering prenatal education, the clients had an opportunity to get to know the doulas, and now 95% of participants accept their services.

For this program, participants allowing doulas to be present at birth is considered an important outcome.

Within prenatal and parenting groups, doulas help their clients build a natural social support system. They connect the girls with the broader community by serving as liaisons to community and health care resources. They accompany clients to prenatal clinic appointments and encourage them to actively participate. One doula asks teens to write three questions for their doctor to take to each prenatal appointment. Some clients express pleasant surprise when their health care providers actually respond positively to their more active involvement in prenatal care. Doulas also serve as translators for their clients, sometimes in a literal sense when a language barrier exists, but also by explaining medical procedures and jargon. It can be daunting for a young mother or someone with limited English to communicate with medical providers. The gentle encouragement of the doula can help her reach beyond her usual comfort zone.

Belly Casting

One creative approach to helping clients focus on their babies while also gaining trust in the doula is belly casting, the creation of a model of a pregnant woman's belly using plaster. Bonnie describes how it works:

> The girls really enjoy belly casting. And both of the doulas enjoy doing it, and we've had such neat experiences. Bina makes it into an arts and crafts activity—she's glued lace trim, and we've had the girls paint them and decorate them. The process of making the belly cast helps to build the teen and doula's relationship and form a connection between the teen and her doula. It validates the teen's pregnancy and helps make it real. Many of our teen moms have difficulty with someone physically touching them because of their own personal histories. Belly casting is good because it is a loving, nurturing touch. It can be powerful for the teen because she is giving permission to have someone touch her body.

Birthing Support

Simple acts such as eye contact, handholding, and words of encouragement—simple but powerful words such as "you can do it" or "you're so strong"—may be the extent of support that some laboring women desire. The doula responds to each client's needs, using her experience, combined with her observational skills, such as sensitivity to body language and facial expressions and a capacity to listen. Attention to the clients' needs is an art. Doulas must attend to the expressed needs of their clients, but they must also use their skills at observation and deduction to identify other needs. Although these skills are emphasized in doula training, the most effective doulas bring innate capacities for listening and observing to their work.

A newly trained doula is likely to feel eager to apply her new knowledge of comfort measures and the other skills she learned in doula training. She dedicates herself to mastering techniques of optimal positioning, massage, relaxation, and breathing, and she stocks her doula bag with an array of products: lotions, massage tools, birth balls (large rubber balls to sit on during labor), and other items. Often the laboring mother welcomes these techniques and tools in the skilled hands of her doula. However, sometimes the doula may be surprised, especially at first, to have clients whose overwhelming need is not for physical comfort measures but for the doula's simple presence, the reassurance that her continuous support can offer.

> It's not about what you want. It's not about what you know best. Yeah, you may know some techniques like massaging or distracting them from the pain. You can take their minds to different places. You learn that over the years; you don't come in knowing that. When you come in as a doula your first instinct is, "Oooh, I can help them. I can do this. I. I. I." Later it's not I.... It's not what I can do for you; it's how have I learned to help you without enforcing all my views. The most you can help a person is when you step back and realize what they want and can give them what they want rather than what you want to give them. (Loretha)

One outcome associated with the continuous supportive presence of a doula is reduced rates of epidural analgesia. Wandy describes such an experience:

> This was the client's third child. She had no doula before, and with those two she had an epidural. After the birth, while she was breastfeeding her baby, she called her friend. She told her, "I had my baby, and I had an epidoula." Her friend said, "you mean an epidural?" "No. I had an epidoula. This time I had a doula. She helped me manage my pain, and it was a great

experience. So, when you have a baby, you should have an epidoula."

Doula Challenges

Doulas also experience many challenges in common, including maintaining boundaries, coping with the intensity of the work, dealing with the hospital—including turf battles—overcoming family resistance, and supporting the young mother's choices.

Boundaries

Community-based doulas may face, or have faced, many of the family and financial stresses experienced by their clients. When doulas come from the communities they serve, they, too, may be struggling with issues related to survival and community violence. Some may face frequent personal crises. However, it may be just these life experiences that enable them to be such effective agents of support for other women in difficult circumstances.

One of doulas' greatest strengths is that they can identify so closely with their clients' lives and their struggles and are so successful in building trusting relationships with them. However, such identification can also be an occupational hazard. Doulas may need guidance to sort out their responses to clients and their roles as support people. Setting boundaries and limits can be difficult as a result of such close personal identification and the empathy that so often characterizes women who choose this work:

> All my clients want to make me a crutch. As much as I love her, there's a line I have to draw. I've got to pull back. You can't be effective if you're too close. (Earnestine)

Being so intimately involved in the lives of the women and their families contributes to stress. Doulas relate stories of clients who face myriad challenges: being homeless or wards of the state, having no money to buy items such as cribs for their babies, moving frequently to live with a series of friends or family members, living with mothers who abuse drugs or steal from them, being victimized by violence. One doula describes a teen client who had lived in 26 foster homes since the age of 5. According to Bonnie:

> You have to prevent yourself from going through vicarious trauma. You have to have that skill to be able to separate. Otherwise you're going to take the work home and wear yourself out. You're going to burn out. [The ability to separate] is a skill the doulas learn very quickly. Because it's a survival skill for them.

Coping With the Intensity

"My longest birth was 48 hours. On my way home, I was praying, 'God, please let my children be good today; mommy's really tired' " (Wandy). Doulas frequently experience both physical and emotional exhaustion from the intense, demanding nature of their work. The work requires sacrifice, plain and simple. In addition to attending very long labors, at times they have had more than one birth on the same day, births 2 days in a row, or even more than one client in labor at the same time. They are on call 24/7, with all the uncertainty that accompanies being permanently on call. Birth is unpredictable, and a doula is often awakened in the middle of the night. Family members may also have their sleep disturbed. As one doula says, "The whole family is involved when there's a doula in the home." Doulas are also away from their families for long or unknown periods of time, and miss special occasions, including holidays, birthdays, and other celebrations. And they must make special arrangements when they have young children. Those without strong family support are under great pressure.

Being part of a team and having adequate backup for births can make an enormous difference in the doula's capacity to continue in this role. Some agencies provide structure by suggesting a maximum number of hours that doulas should remain at the hospital. Others leave that up to the discretion of individual doulas, believing that experienced doulas will recognize their own limits and assess when they need help from a backup doula. Some doulas are determined to remain at the laboring woman's side, regardless of the length of her labor. Some welcome relief from a backup doula, perhaps for a brief period of rest, and say that they would surely burn out if they had no backup. Some doulas who have left their jobs say unequivocally that it was because of a lack of support in this area.

Doulas develop coping mechanisms for the emotional intensity of the work. One of the most essential practices is talking with others about the births they attend and reflecting on what happened, especially when it was unusually stressful or traumatic. It is particularly comforting for doulas to process the birth experiences with other doulas, as Loretha shares:

> Some people, if they haven't been trained in labor and delivery, you could tell them that the girl had an episiotomy. They don't know what you're talking about. Now if you just say, "she split like a chicken," they might understand that, but they don't want to hear it. Nobody wants to hear that. So that's a language that only a doula can understand. When you talk to other doulas, when they listen to your words, it's like they're putting their arms around you. It's like "tell me more." But you don't have to use too many words to explain what happened. You just say two or three words, and they say, "Girl, I know. I was at births like that."

> ...You have to talk to other doulas. As far as the wear and tear on your body and the amount that it messes with your psyche, only another doula can understand that....You can unload, just dump everything you need to dump out and clear your head with one of the veteran doulas. They play a vital role in whether you go crazy or stay sane.

Sometimes doulas need repeated chances to tell their stories. Witnessing events that feel like a violation of their clients can be profoundly disturbing. A doula may feel intensely helpless as she observes procedures and treatment that seem unnecessary, intrusive, or disrespectful.

Doulas describe many situations in which their young clients were treated with indifference, disrespect, or even hostility. They hear disparaging remarks and observe obstetrical procedures performed without explanation. In an environment in which their own status often feels precarious, it is painful and challenging for the doulas to cope with hostility expressed by health care providers toward the teens:

> For me, when I see them mistreating someone, what I started doing was reporting them. And I was like oh "holy terror" when I came up on the floor. But I didn't care, because I kept saying, "Okay, now when you see me and you see that she's with me, you will not—by no means—disrespect her." … If you're going to advocate for [your clients] you don't do it when it's convenient for you. Do it no matter what happens. At first they look at you as a troublemaker, but then they turn around and look at you with respect. (Tikvah)

The doula is mindful of the delicate line she walks. If she objects too forcefully, she may be told to leave, and she knows that her continuous presence and support is essential to her client's well- being.

Another situation that can devastate doulas is when a baby dies. Doulas speak heart-wrenchingly about supporting women in labor who deliver a stillborn baby or being there for a new mother whose baby died of sudden infant death syndrome (SIDS). Doulas say that no amount of preparation is adequate for this experience. Although they had participated in discussions of this topic during and after doula training and had been exposed to testimonials and literature describing various experiences of loss, actually confronting the loss of a baby is both a personal and professional challenge.

It is critical to the long-term ability of doulas to function in this role and avoid burnout that they debrief with others who also speak their language. Otherwise, doulas are likely to feel overwhelmed by the intensity of this work.

Dealing With the Hospital

One of the more challenging aspects of the doulas' work in the hospital is gaining access to their clients. Doulas experience a range of situations as they attempt to gain access to hospital units. Some doulas attend births at as many as 10 different hospitals. Some are employed by an agency with close ties to one hospital and may even be issued an employee ID, which obviously simplifies access. However, even these doulas may still experience difficulty gaining access to their clients in certain areas of the labor and delivery unit, such as the obstetrical triage area, where doulas have sometimes been required to wait outside while the client is first evaluated. One doula recalls:

> I got the call for this birth, and I've never been at this hospital before. As I was driving there, I was just praying, "Please, God, don't let this hospital give me trouble." I know that this girl's really going to need me at her birth, and I hope that they let me up there. And that the nurses treat me decent so that I can help her. (Anonymous)

Doulas express frustration and concern for their clients as the teens make their first transition from the outside to the hospital setting. In addition to the personal frustration and disappointment doulas experience when they are denied access to their laboring clients, they also worry about how this affects the teens, especially in terms of the effect of laboring unsupported. This is a particularly stressful time for the teens, especially if they're in active labor and not able to receive support from their doula.

There are other reasons why doulas are unable to attend births. One common experience is denial of access to the operating room when the client has a cesarean section. Doulas tell of spending long hours supporting a laboring client, only to be left behind when she has a cesarean. On some occasions, plans fall through, and the teen does not have arrangements for transportation to the hospital when she is in labor. She may call an ambulance and be taken to the nearest hospital, where the doula is not expected or familiar to hospital staff; this can increase the challenge of gaining access. Doulas also are disappointed when they learn that their clients go to the hospital without even attempting to notify them. Some teens lose the phone number; others' labor progresses more quickly than expected. For some, the teen's mother doesn't want the doula to be called. At times, there is no explanation.

Doulas worry about the possible effect on the teen's trust of the doula if they are separated at the hospital. Loretha says:

> They ask me, "Who are you, her mom?" I hesitate. I want to say yes, cause I know that would get me back there; that's an instant ticket. They say, "You're not her mom, then you'll have to wait. We'll come back and let you know when you can come back." So this is the part that's really frustrating to me because my thing is, once I promise my girls that I'm never going to leave them, then they believe me. And that's part of the trust. Now I've broken that trust by leaving her. She's thinking about that....

At times, hospital staff consider the doula a visitor, and they deny her entry to the room if the allotted number of visitors is already present. Familiarizing nurses with the doula's role and purpose is made more difficult by frequent turnover in nursing staff.

Turf battles. Despite the growing popularity of doulas—especially private practice doulas—and the hospital staff's increasing familiarity with them, community-based doulas often face suspicion or even overt hostility. This occurs for a number of reasons. Those unfamiliar with the doula's purely supportive, non-clinical role may mistakenly perceive her as a threat to their jobs, believing that the doula's practice might invade their professional territory. This contributes to a sense of turf wars.

Doulas acting within their scope of practice complement the functions of nurses and doctors and work collaboratively in such a way that enhances the experience of childbirth. A fundamental principle we emphasize in doula training is the scope and limits of doula practice. Doulas understand that their role is to educate the client and encourage her to speak on her own behalf—to find her own voice. It is the doula's role to inform clients of their choices, and encourage them to ask questions. Although doulas do not directly confront nurses or doctors, health care providers sometimes see them as confrontational women who overstep their boundaries in their role as patient advocates, either by explicitly advising clients about clinical decisions, such as refusing medical interventions, or by directly opposing medical and nursing professionals. If a practitioner has had a previous negative experience with a doula, it can prove daunting for the community-based doula to win acceptance, at least initially.

Doulas are keenly aware of their own precarious acceptance and understand that they are of no value to the teen if they are forced to leave her side. By being patient and nondefensive and by demonstrating their value to the laboring mother and as a member of the team—one with a nonclinical role—doulas generally are successful over time in overcoming this resistance.

Tikvah writes about her challenges being accepted by medical and nursing staff at a large urban hospital and about her efforts and eventual success at gaining their trust. She imagines her client's entrance to the hospital:

> The green canopy, up the steps past the guard—as she approaches the long hallway to labor and delivery, she also approaches her grand entrance of motherhood. As her emotions and hormones are racing, she remains calm, because she has her doula with her. Right? Wrong! The door opens and closes; it receives the mother to be, but not the doula. I could only imagine what is going on in her mind, what is going on with her body. Are they talking her through every step while they're examining her? Who's holding her hand? Who's calming her fears? Who's commending her on her breathing techniques? I could only imagine!
>
> We're starting to have a better relationship with them.... At first, it was like we were taking their jobs. But we didn't give up! We're working as a team,

the doctors, nurses, patients, and the doulas. We have a common goal; that
is to help this mother have a memorable birth and help with the bonding
process. Now they embrace us, and I look at them more now as allies than
I did before. We know that we have had some challenges in the beginning....
But we keep in mind that the biggest thing is not how you begin; it's how
you finish.

Community-based doulas become savvy in combining diplomacy and advocacy.
Discussions and role-plays in doula training about their uncertain welcome by
health care providers results in strategic interactions with staff. Bonnie, for
example, explains that she and the other doulas were prepared for this perception of the doula as adversarial or confrontational: "We knew that going in because
of the doula training, so we low-key it."

Hospital routines. Doulas who practice in the hospital setting, whether private practice or community based, often express great frustration with hospital-
imposed limitations on their ability to function fully as doulas. This often is due
to routine policies resulting in women's confinement to bed and procedures such
as continuous fetal monitoring, increasingly frequent induction of labor, epidural
analgesia, and cesarean section. In recent years, there have been dramatic increases
in rates of most of these obstetrical interventions. This often results in both the
laboring woman and her doula feeling constrained in the measures they can implement for comfort and in their ability to labor without interference.

However, community-based doulas understand that they have no control over
medical decisions, and so they focus on their core role. They are at the birth to
provide emotional support and comfort to the mother and to help her have the
most positive birth experience she can. As one program director says:

If the doula is too upset, she can't be emotionally and physically supportive of the mother. She won't be able to focus her energy and passion. So,
she has to prioritize.

However, she concedes that these situations can be difficult for her doulas, and she explains the importance of providing ample opportunities following the birth to express their feelings.

Family Resistance

At times, family members, especially the teen's mother, are responsible for denying the doula access to her client in labor. Loretha tells a painful story:

> The grandmother called me that she was on her way down to switch places with me. She said, "Wait right there, and I'll be down in a minute." So, I'm waiting, and three security guys walked up to me and told me, "You have to leave the hospital." And I'm trying to figure out why, and I asked them why, and they said, "by request of the grandma." And I said, "I have to hear it from the grandma," because according to our rules, we can't just leave— just because security says I'm not needed on a birth. I needed to hear it from the participant or her mother. I asked, "Can I wait here 'til the grandma gets down here?" And they said, "No, we have instructions to ask you to get out of the hospital."

When asked how she managed to cope with this experience and to continue working with this grandmother, Loretha replies:

> After all the doula training, I was taught not to take things personally, and I had to go there. For whatever their reasons are, it's not personal.... Some people can't express their feelings. They either lash out with their words or sometimes with their actions. You just learn not to take it personally, because if you do ... it's going to eat away at you. You'll never ever figure out why. The only things you can do are take a step back and try to allow that person to come back. And nine times out of ten, they do come back.

Another situation in which the family may interfere with the doula's work is in relation to breastfeeding:

Girls say that they want to breastfeed, and you have all these family members in the room. And the nurse says how are you feeding the baby, and you're saying, "yeah, yeah, yeah," and she says "no," and you say, "But I thought you were going to breastfeed?" And she says, "But my mother said I can't." This is not the time to pick a fight because she has to go home with her mom....

But if she says she definitely wants to breastfeed no matter what her family says, then I'm gonna stick with her. And if I have to go up against those family members knowing that I might not be invited to the house when she comes home, then I have to take that chance... I'm going to stick with her. I tell the father or the grandmother, "This is what she wants. Let's just try to support her. Maybe we can just try a couple of weeks. And if after a couple of weeks if the baby doesn't like it or she's uncomfortable with it, then we'll talk again." (Loretha)

Supporting the Young Mother's Choice

A challenging aspect of doula work is supporting a client's choice even when the doula has a different view. A doula provides her client information about an array of topics, including choices in childbirth, breastfeeding, circumcision, and so forth, and then steps back to allow her to make an informed choice. Being non-judgmental is an underlying principle, a foundation upon which the doula can build a long-term trusting relationship with her client. The importance of remaining nonjudgmental is explored at length in doula training.

Now sometimes if the girl says, "I want an epidural," and you remind them, "Are you sure this is what you want? Remember you said you didn't want this." And they say, "I don't care. I'm hurting too bad." And you have to step back and say, "This is not my birth, so why am I taking it so personally?" This is what she wants, then this is what she's going to get. But these are things you have to learn to deal with.... I've changed throughout the years. It's their birth; it's their decision. I support them, and I'm there for them. I totally respect that now. (Loretha)

Doulas' Perceptions of Their Effect

"They grab you and they won't let go." (Lovie)

Over the years, doulas have shared the assorted names their clients use to refer to them and the ways the teens describe their role:

People Call Us...

Douley

Mama Doula

The Birth Ladies

Dola

Doma

Douhallie

Labor Person

Help Futter Birth

Ma' Doula

Veteran Doula

Mary Doula

Abdulla

Auntie Doula

Lady Who Help You Have Your Baby

Epidoula

And Say We Are ...

Marriage Counselor

Teacher

Older Sister

Taxi Driver

Friend

Mother

Lawyer

Know-It-All

Nurse

Midwife

Comadrona

Case Manager

It is obvious from the doulas' stories that clients regard them as women who wear many hats. Many become deeply attached to their doulas. "We're not professional social workers or psychologists, but tell that to the client." (Earnestine) Michele, a program coordinator, talks about one doula's experience:

> Joy was a 19-year-old client expecting her second baby. As her pregnancy
> neared the end, she had almost daily contact with Cassandra.... Cassandra
> attended the birth, and it went very well. Cassandra continued to make home
> visits to support Joy's breastfeeding and care of the new baby, and Joy called
> Cassandra almost daily. Because the family moved out of the attendance
> area, Cassandra let Joy know that she would have to be ending at about 6
> weeks. At a home visit, she reminded Joy and her partner that next week
> would be her last visit, stating that they should make plans for a special good-
> bye. Joy burst into tears, sobbing that she had hoped that Cassandra would
> be the baby's unofficial grandmother.

Negotiating these global expectations and clarifying role boundaries are essential for doulas and their supervisors. Every doula struggles to find a balance in
her intensely personal and professional relationships.

Doulas describe changes in the teens they work with, both in terms of their own
self-image and their mothering behaviors:

> They seem more confident, more comfortable with their babies. More able
> to show the love that they're feeling. They have a greater desire to nurture
> their babies. More of our girls at least attempt breastfeeding. We see bet-
> ter mother–child attachment. I have no doubt about that. That's how I meas-
> ure the success of the program. That is, not only do we have the attended
> births and increased breastfeeding and decreased epidurals and decreased
> C-sections. Those things are kind of obvious. But to me, the thing is, do we
> have better mother–child attachment? Is this mother feeling more confident
> about being a new mom, is she closer to her baby, is she bonding with her
> baby well? ....It's not something you can measure that easily. But I see it.
> (Bonnie)

Another important possibility is that doulas may help to reduce the risk of postpartum depression, as some research has demonstrated. One program adminis-
trator, Juana, reports that teen mothers are more available emotionally to their

babies since the doula program was added to her agency. Juana and her colleagues also believe that there has been less postpartum depression in the teens receiving doula services in contrast to those who only have home visitors. The implications of this are significant: depression contributes to reduced availability and responsiveness by mothers.

Two Doula Stories

The following two stories capture the continuing experience of the doula–teen relationship, as described by community-based doulas Tracy and Bina.

Tracy describes an experience with a 14-year-old client that she called a pivotal moment for her:

> This experience showed me not to judge my work by the moment. The time I invest in the present may have dividends in the future even though I may never know them.

Tracy's story also reveals her capacity to be flexible and nondefensive, even in the face of her client's refusal of services.

> Of the many stories I have as a doula, the one that stands out this summer began last summer. It involved my youngest client ever (under 15) and the important lessons she taught me. One of my job descriptions includes weekly home visits, but she did not want this. So I suggested we meet at a neutral location, a park near her house. However, she stood me up on one of the hottest days of summer.
>
> .... When I wasn't called for the birth there was disappointment, but I learned to respect personal choice. Another requirement of my job is to stay in weekly contact with the mom for 3 months after the birth. Since the mom was difficult to reach by relatives' cell phones, I wrote her letters and sent post-

cards, and occasionally I would see her and the baby at the clinic, where we would talk about her, the baby, and motherhood.

But I'll never forget when 3 or more months after our required contact she stopped by the office and stayed over 2 hours, just talking about many things in her past and present. I was amazed. I'm not sure it if was because I was simply available or something more…. when she called me some months later, it was just before the baby's first birthday, and I was very happy to hear from her. We chatted briefly, and I asked her to go out with me on Saturday. She agreed, and I met her at the park where she had stood me up over a year ago. I brought my two sons, and off we went. We not only went to the museum but the zoo, also. As we explored the museum I mentioned that the children we see play in water today are future plumbers and engineers of tomorrow. She commented on the fact that there were a lot of blond children in the museum, and I agreed with her, sharing that often people of color are under-represented in museums. I'm so used to this that it was surprising to hear it mentioned. I hope the museum and zoo day inspired this young mom to do that in the future. I wonder about the effect on the child, but I can't see way down the line.

Tracy added that she liked to think that this experience would inspire this young mother to provide more opportunities for her child to learn and expand her worldview. Tracy's story shows the doula as liaison to the wider world and highlights her potential to enlarge the client's capacity for experience. Tracy expresses hope for this young mother and her child, and that hope is one important aspect of the work that sustains the doulas. Unlike a private practice doula whose relationship with her client is brief and whose focus is on facilitating a positive birth experience, the community-based doula has a vision of making a long-term effect on the young mothers' lives, on their aspirations for themselves and their children.

Bina describes dramatic changes in one of her youngest clients as a result of her involvement and their relationship, in which trust—and therefore the doula's influence—grew over time:

When I first met this young 14-year-old girl, she seemed very serious. She was 5 months pregnant, but the fundus was the size of a 2- or 3-month expectant mom. She said that she only weighs 101 pounds and that the doctor is concerned. We discussed the importance of nutrition for her and her developing baby. I asked her to tell me what she had for breakfast. She said, "I haven't had anything to eat yet." I said, "You need to eat breakfast; you need to eat something." We discussed the fetal brain, organs, and growth and development. She finally said, "We do not have a refrigerator; that is why we don't have any food in the house. We've been without a refrigerator for over a month. The landlord keeps promising that he will replace it but never does." I suggested they call the Health Department.

I felt a gradual trust happening. She's beginning to understand that I was there to support her and that the questions I asked were because I was concerned and not just being nosey. She was making me earn her trust. At the next visit I asked again about the refrigerator. Still no refrigerator. I suggested they get a cooler and ice and store food in it, and I stressed nutrition again.

The following week she told me that they got a cooler; that now she has some food to eat. She asked if I would call the Health Department to complain about their situation, and I gladly did. They said they would see the landlord within 2 days.

At my next visit, I could see her lips as she greeted me with a big smile and invited me in. She said, "We have a refridge. The landlord brought it on the third day after you called." And she proceeded to tell me a list of food items she had in it.

A relationship is already happening. I have earned it! I asked if she had been going for walks. She said, "No, I am too embarrassed to go outside." I asked, "Why?" She said, "Because I am pregnant. I am too embarrassed, because people will stare at me and wonder what is this young kid doing pregnant?

I want the baby, Bina, but I don't want to be pregnant." I said, "You are pregnant, and it is your baby—and don't worry about what people think. Let's work on getting your baby to grow." I asked her, "How do you think the baby feels about her mom being embarrassed of the baby being in her tummy?" She said, "I will try and work on that, Bina."

The visits are going much better. She tells me that she can't sleep, that she is afraid to go to sleep and that she stays up all night. I asked her why. She said, "Because the baby is MESSING WITH ME. Every night I have the same dream where she sticks her hand out of my vagina and wants to grab me. Then she pulls her hand back in or she sticks her head out, makes faces at me, then pops it back in." She said, "It's too scary, Bina." I suggested she should talk to the baby and tell her how much she loves her, caress her tummy, sing and read to her baby, write letters to her baby, play soft and relaxing music. I suggested to start showing off her tummy and to be proud of her baby; the baby will be happy and feel loved. She agreed to do it.

On the following visits, she starts to show me her tummy and how big her belly is now. We both grin from ear to ear with pride. There are no more complaints of sleepless nights.

She has lots of questions. Some I answer, and some I suggest she make a list of and ask her doctor at her next prenatal appointment. She said she was too scared to talk. I told her that doctors like it when patients ask a lot of questions about their health. I told her, "This will show them how intelligent you are, that you ask very good questions." She said, "Ok, Bina."

I went to pick her up for her prenatal appointment. I was so proud and impressed when she started asking the doctor questions and clarifications regarding her previous visits and about her baby's health. When we stepped out of the room, she looked at me and said, "This is so weird. The doctor was so different today." I said, "No, honey. It wasn't the doctor that was different, it was you because you asked all those good questions, and the doctor was happy to answer them."

Initially, she said that she definitely did not want to breastfeed. I respected her decision but still explained the benefits. During an afternoon home visit, my cell phone rang, and a sweet voice said, "Bina, I am in the hospital, and they are going to do a C-section because the placenta is separating." I said, "I am on my way." Due to other circumstances, the C-section was delayed, and I took the opportunity to talk to her about the benefits of the MIRA-CLE DRINK for the baby, HER BREAST MILK. She was only in her 29th week. She agreed to pump. The baby weighed 2.5 lbs. This young mom was so dedicated, every day she filled many containers and would relate to me every week how many ounces her baby had gained. At times she would say, "Bina, the baby is so small." I would say, "But you are giving your baby the best gift a mother can give to her baby; she will grow. Just keep saying, 'My baby is going to make it!'"

I asked her, "How does it feel to be a mommy?" She says that motherhood is beginning to kick in. She told me that one of the nurses in the NICU was telling her baby, "Hey, you stupid baby, wake up," when the baby was in sleep apnea. I asked her, "What did you do to protect your baby from this nurse?" She said, "I wasn't sure I was hearing right and when she said it again I said, 'What are you saying to my baby?' and the nurse stopped." The mom told me, "Those nurses think I am stupid just because I am so young." She said, "When the baby was transferred to this hospital I told them my baby is on breast milk, but they wouldn't listen to me until the baby started vomiting the formula. Then they started the baby back on breast milk."

The nurse told her that the baby might be discharged in time for Mother's Day. What a special gift, due to mother's milk! The following week I went to visit her, and the baby was home! I asked her, "Are you getting enough sleep? How often does the baby wake to feed?" She said, "She wakes up about three times during the night, but she falls back to sleep right after I nurse her." My eyes opened wide as I asked her to please repeat what she just said. She actually said NURSING. I asked, "How did you do it? Does the baby latch on ok?" She said, "Yes, 1 week before the baby came home

I told the nurse that I will breastfeed when I get home, and the good nurse said, 'Honey, you better start right now before you go home. Otherwise you might have some difficulty getting the baby to latch on.' So the nurse helped me." I congratulated her on what a great mom she is and how proud I am of her. My teeth had never been this exposed before as I smiled for miles to my next home visit!

Rewards

The effect of doula work is not just on the clients. The lives of the doulas are also changed. Although the work is challenging, the rewards can be profound:

Being a doula ... This has helped accentuate who I really am, how strong I am. And how the more we give, the more we receive. Because these kids that we support give us so much love and respect, no matter what age we are. We know when we're doing our work because it shows in our girls— when they call us, when they cancel so we don't have to come and nobody's there. When they call us when it's time to go to the hospital. We grow; WE grow by the girls accepting us. We're all the same. So we just go there as human beings. We don't go as Hispanics or African Americans or Caucasians. We're just human beings. To me, it has deepened my respect, the love for humanity, knowing that we are one... Every birth, every girl is different. THEY teach us something about ourselves. And that is the beauty of growing; we do change. I feel that I have changed for the better. I have grown in many, many ways. (Bina)

Rosalba describes the effect of the work on her life:

I feel that my life would have been different if I would not have experienced childbirth as a teenager myself. This has placed me in the shoes of the young and naïve teenager. My experience is very deep, and it is hard to explain it well in words. I have doula instincts, doula insight, and doula wisdom. I can remember my first birth when I learned for the first time that I can make a difference with my presence. To this date, I still feel the same at every birth I attend. Knowing I can empower young women gives me strength as a doula. Being a doula has made me a better person, because I have learned so much from every birth.

The doulas provide their clients with guidance and positive energy, encouraging them to believe that they can be successful. Doulas also tell them that they don't have to stay in negative living situations or relationships. For some doulas, this identification with clients and their heightened awareness about the parallels to their own lives has resulted in a new perspective—and also in personal change. Some are concluding:

We can do it as well, and we begin to emerge. I'm always telling my teen moms that they can do it; well so can I. It will be a challenge, but I can succeed.

For some, this has resulted in doulas getting counseling or leaving abusive partners. For others, it has meant being a woman with a stronger voice who is more capable of asserting herself in relationships and in her work.

When speaking about the changes she has observed, a doula supervisor says:

She has done an incredible amount of growth. She has been able to trust her own professionalism. She has gotten a voice for herself. She's been empowered herself. (Bonnie)

One experienced doula trainer notes:

For many women, doula training is the beginning of a life transformation. During training they begin to explore their capacities, their potential, their power. Once they have an opportunity to practice, they not only are aware but they begin to act on their awareness. They begin to speak their minds

with the mothers they work with, then with medical providers, then with
their family members and school staff. They begin to practice making
change at work, and that translates into making change at home. They begin
to change the way they look by cutting their hair, wearing bright colors, wearing jewelry or lipstick. This translates to how other people perceive them.
Others begin to describe them as strong, opinionated, colorful, interesting,
powerful, determined. People describe them even as taller, more athletic,
more articulate than they even are, probably because of the confidence the
doula exudes. People believe they can do even more than they are capable
of doing. They are seen as superwomen, and sometimes they begin to believe
it. (Jere)

For many community-based doulas, the rewards of their work are in the satisfaction they derive from knowing that they have changed young women's lives.
Their effect extends beyond guiding their clients through successful birthing and
breastfeeding experiences. For many doulas, rewards of a job well done are in helping young mothers understand that "there is a light; they can get beyond the dark
tunnel," that is, they can fulfill their potential by educating themselves and their
babies, learning English as a second language, completing their GED, returning to school, striving for more. As one doula says when reflecting on the effect
of this work on her personally as well as on her teen clients, "This is about being
someone for ourselves." Through encouraging the teens' personal growth, their
own growth has been enhanced. Working as doulas has been transformative for
many, both in terms of educational and professional aspirations and in terms of
finding a more powerful inner voice and a stronger self-image of their value and
their possibilities.

In the words of Lovie Griffin, doula supervisor:

To be a doula is a challenge we are given.

A gift we must accept.

A tragedy we sometimes are faced with.

A duty we must perform.

Mysteries we must watch unfold.

A song that we have to sing.

An opportunity we dare not miss.

A journey we must complete.

Love we must realize.

A struggle to fight so that we can achieve life's goals.

References

Cardone, I., Gilkerson, L., & Wechsler, N. (in press). *The Community-Based FANA*. Washington, DC: ZERO TO THREE Press.

Klaus, M. H., Kennell, J. H., Klaus, P. H. (2002). *The doula book: How a trained labor companion can help you have a shorter, easier, and healthier birth.* Cambridge, MA: Perseus Publishing.

Chapter 7

Listening to the Voices of Young Mothers: Women's Experience of Doula Support

Any assessment of a new program model would be incomplete without including the experience of program participants. This is particularly important in complex, relationship-based service models. A number of studies have demonstrated the effect of doula support during labor on enhanced maternal self-esteem, maternal–infant bonding, and increased satisfaction with the birth experience in adult women (Hemminki et al.,1990; Hofmeyr et al., 1991; Orenstein, 1998). However, only one published study describes mothers' experiences when receiving consistent, extended doula care during pregnancy, labor and delivery, and the early postpartum weeks (Breedlove, 2005).

This chapter includes narrative quotes from participants in two descriptive studies (Breedlove, 2001, 2004, 2005) that reflect the voices of teen program participants in the Chicago Doula Project. These excerpts describe themes that emerged from individual interviews and a focus group session.

Findings of both studies support the importance of the ongoing, relationship-based caring provided by community-based doulas. Participant interviews supported earlier findings in adult populations that the presence of a doula enhances young mothers' feeling of emotional support and care, provides modeling of early attachment behavior with the newborn, and increases mothers' self-confidence. We conclude by describing essential characteristics of the doula that participants described as contributing significantly to their feeling that they are "stronger women" because of their doula support in the past and continuing friendships today.

A Qualitative Study

In 2001, 30 pregnant or parenting teens living on the West Side of Chicago were involved in a study investigating the effect of the Chicago Doula Project (Breedlove, 2001, 2004, 2005). This descriptive, qualitative study was designed to explore and describe the perception of social support and hope in teens who had received support from a community-based doula during pregnancy, labor and birth, and the postpartum period. The study addressed eight research questions:

- How do teen moms describe networks and individuals that provide assistance and support?

- What supportive characteristics by the doula are described during pregnancy, labor and birth, and early mothering?

- How is support from the doula different than other types of described support?

- What factors determine whether additional support is desired?

- How is the support valued?

- What is the perception of hope by the teen for her future?

- What is described as necessary internal and external resources to actualize her future goals?

- How did the relationship with a doula affect her level of hope?

Methods

The researcher interviewed participating teens over a period of 9 months in 2001. Two groups were recruited: pregnant teens who were receiving doula services prenatally and anticipated the presence of a doula during labor and birth, and parenting teens who were now mothering who had received support from a doula during pregnancy and labor and birth, through 6 weeks postdelivery. Twelve pregnant and 12 parenting teen mothers met eligibility criteria and participated in this study after consent was obtained. Participants in the program were African American teens between the ages of 14 and 18, were Medicaid recipients, and were receiving doula services from one of the pilot sites for the Chicago Doula Project.

This same community agency has provided various supportive services in the West Side of Chicago in a disadvantaged neighborhood for over 50 years. The project director of the doula program, a social worker, has been involved in the lives of many of the participants for over 15 years, supervising some of the mothers when they were younger in the youth risk prevention program and now as pregnant teens involved in the doula program. Doulas at this agency were employed full time as part of a broader teen support program. They were assigned a monthly caseload of teens to provide one-on-one support through early pregnancy, rotate 24-hour call to attend births, and provide follow-up home visiting up to 6 weeks postpartum. All doulas were involved, along with other staff, in prenatal and postdelivery educational sessions.

Results

Results reported for purposes of this book are combined findings from both pregnant and parenting teens. Using qualitative study methodology, a number of significant themes emerged to describe the unique and important role the community-based doula plays. These included:

• Providing education during pregnancy and parenting;

• Providing emotional support;

- Maintaining continued presence and support in labor, birth, and early parenting;

- Supporting orientation toward a brighter future;

- Providing encouragement to succeed;

- Modeling positive parenting behaviors; and

- Encouraging breastfeeding initiation.

The following narratives excerpts from participant interviews provide evidence of these significant themes.

Education for pregnancy and parenting preparation. Various educational programs facilitated by the doulas—taught individually and in groups—provided teens opportunities to learn more about prenatal issues, choices in childbirth preparation and birth, effective parenting, and initiation of breastfeeding. Groups were facilitated by trained women residing within the community. All of the teens described the educational sessions as the primary support from the doulas during their pregnancy and later in the postpartum period. Educational content was provided during weekly group sessions, with an emphasis on pregnancy and early parenting topics. Additionally, doulas made personal phone calls, home visits, and encouraged individual discussion related to sensitive topics. Doulas also provided community resource information important to the mothers, including how to access Special Supplementary Food Programs for Women, Infants, and Children (WIC), transportation vouchers for prenatal care, and neighborhood GED programs.

Health education included both mother-focused and baby-focused information. In describing education classes, one mother shared the following,

> ...They give you good things and how basically you are suppose to raise a child ... and how to be a better mom. They help you out quite a bit.

Basically we had groups once a week, once or twice, I don't remember…and they would encourage us to breastfeed and ask us questions about how you can develop your child's brain while she was still in your stomach, and they would teach us to read to the baby now and how to play with her…. you sing to your baby and play soft music. The prenatal class or whatever that we watched videos of women in labor … and talked about breathing techniques and like … the position that you want to be in while you are having a baby, like in the tub or on your knees or on your back whichever you feel comfortable, and then like the group, once you started group, then they talk about parenting.

Emotional Support. Emotional support provided by the doulas to the mothers emerged as a strong theme for both pregnant and parenting teens: "They was like somebody to come and talk to you, they told you what to do, what not to do, they were basically like a mother." Another mother shared:

It was like me being 16 and being pregnant … you could be having a real bad day, or whatever, and feeling down and let's say you scheduled for a doula meeting and visit that day and once you sit down and talk about things and whatever about your problems you notice that well, I'm not alone. You feel much better, you know, and that is what they have done for me. That it's not as hard as everybody makes it seem and they say they're going to be there for us, that we be having the baby and that they're there to help us, they won't make you feel so down about your mistake.

One mother expressed how much she appreciated not being judged:

It made it easier to me, because I didn't think, you know, I got pregnant at 15 so … I didn't think people would be so supportive. You know, they wasn't downing me or anything like that. They made me feel better about my pregnancy because at first I was depressed.

Continuity of support in labor, birth, and early parenting. Ongoing contact during and beyond the prenatal period emerged as a significant theme from participants:

> They give me their home phone number. They continued to check on me. They come to your home and make sure you are all right, like when you get further in your months, check on you.... They came by my house to ask me how I was doing, what was the other thing? I believe they were teaching me about exercises that you could do to relieve some of the pressure.

Another mother recalled how the doula's unexpected drop-in visit to her home may have saved her baby's life:

> I missed the doctors appointment and they [doulas] came over ... and they had told me like get up off the couch, we are going to a doctors appointment...so they done took me across the street, and the doctor checked me out, and they gave me an ultrasound, and they discovered there wasn't no water around the baby, and they said they were glad that I had came in, because she probably would have passed away if I wouldn't. They took me over to the hospital then, and they stay with me.

All participants placed a high value on the continuous presence and support of the doulas during the labor and birth experience. As one mother cradled her breast-feeding infant in her arms, she recalled the hard work of labor and the comforting presence of her doula:

> I just couldn't take the pain, so she [the doula] was like trying to comfort me, she brought me ice, and then she snuck in the water cause I was so thirsty. She would massage my legs, my back, comb my hair for me cause I came to the hospital looking like nowhere. She was just really there for me. She was, you know, holding my hand, talking to me, calming me down...she was definitely there.... she helped me to walk down the hall-way—that was hard, because when you are having contractions it is hard to walk, so I went to lay back down; she was just helping me relax. She was

helping me get through it...she keep encouraging me...she made it easier, she calmed me down and made me feel better, she was helping me breathe, giving me ice chips, fanning me, wiping the sweat off, you know. Being there, being there, she helped me feel comfortable, she helped me, she told me just breathe through it, she said just breathe through all the pains, and every time it came (contractions) she was right next to me, showing me how to breathe. So I didn't need medication. No one else did that for me, she knew me and how to help me. I've never had that help before.

After delivery, all participants described supportive care from the home visits provided by the doulas. This included continuing education, teaching skills, and observance of the environment for newborn safety. One mother was surprised by her home visit:

Yeah, all of them ... everybody loved me, everybody came and brought me gifts and stuff and they videotaped me. They scared to tell me they really don't suppose to spend that much time, basically there's so much for them to do. You know, but they likes my family. They talked to me for awhile, you know, checking on me every day. They made me feel good, just to know they was thinking about me.

Orientation toward a brighter future. Another theme that emerged was that doulas support the young mothers' orientation toward a brighter future. Three themes related to perceived hope for the future: desire for a brighter future, achievement of goals, and normalcy of life. Doulas encourage the teens to establish personal goals and to complete their high school education. They help them design a plan to achieve their goals. Hope for a brighter future included the teens' desire for a fulfilling life—to have a better home for self and children, a good job, and enough money not to need welfare. One mother shared:

Hope to me means like knowing that after years of struggling and time and time again, of being, you know, going through something, that there is still something good coming at the end.

Participants clearly expressed hope for the future and described personal confidence:

> I am going to make it. That I am going to stick to my dreams and do what I wanted to do…. I hoped that a lot of the stuff come true, and so far I hoped it and it came true. It's about achieving, achieving, you know, still setting the same goals that I had before I got pregnant. I want to finish high school. I have one more year, and then I want to go to college to study radiology, and actually what I want to do is, you know, do the ultrasound…just to go on with my life and do something better, for her sake and mine…so she can have some of the things that I didn't have growing up.

Participants also described specific areas in which the doulas provided encouragement for a hopeful future:

> Sometimes you will be so down and you discouraged about some of the things you're doing, and I can call [listed the names of all the doulas] and they'll keep pushing me to continue on what it is I'm doing…so they keep pushing me because they know that I might cry, whine or let on, say I'm gonna quit, but they know I'm not going to do it and I know that I'm not gonna act on it.

A newly delivered mother said:

> Like where we live at, there is nothing really positive down there. So you don't think about nothin' positive, and you just live for the day or for whatever happens, but as long as you discuss positive things and work towards it, talk 'bout it, which they [doulas] do, you will think about it.

Providing encouragement to succeed. Doulas provide encouragement to mothers in a number of ways. These include assistance on an as-needed, individual basis; being available in times of crisis; consistency in caring; and believing in the mother's potential to succeed. Supporting examples of these characteristics were derived from comments such as, "They, they really good to talk to, they treat you like, like you are their own kid." One young mother said:

> Ain't all help is good help, but some of it is the best, and I think this [doula program] is the best.

Another shared:

> They done told me to strive for what I want to strive for, and no matter what, let no one take my hopes and my dreams away from me. No one ever encouragin' me like that before.

The doulas provide adult modeling for success. Their personal achievement in enhancing their own lives—being trained and employed as a doula within their community—increases the teens' hope that they, too, can achieve:

> Cause they [doulas] showin' me how to be a better person and to do different things, don't do what other people do, don't be a follower, you know, do your own kinda work that you want to do… And there is lots of doulas here who have been through the same problems that we been through, and they made it, so we can.

Some of the teen participants described personal goals that included becoming a midwife, nurse, breastfeeding peer counselor, doula, or child care provider. Many of those roles had been of direct benefit to participants as they received health care services during their pregnancy and early parenting:

> The doulas they help out teen moms a lot, because I know a lot of teen mothers they struggle a lot and it's really hard to be a mother so young, they been there. They be talking about stuff to help you be better, and I mean you can ask questions…it's gonna help me in the future because I get the answers and I know that later in the future I can always come back up here and ask a question if I need it, and it'll be answered. They tell you

about the facts, and they be real with you, they don't beat around the bush and all the stuff like other programs do. They make sure I was in school, took me to a job fair, and after I have my baby will help me be able to get a job.

Modeling positive parenting behaviors. The knowledge disseminated by the doulas was described as different from the kind of education promoted by other health care providers during the young mothers' childbearing experience. Participants felt that that the doula provided real-life advice and possessed more fact-based knowledge, and that because the doulas had similar life experiences they could better understand the mothers' challenging circumstances. One participant described the doulas' way of emphasizing positive maternal behaviors with her newborn:

Well, like they came when you first had the baby, they came to see you, they talk to you, they hold the baby for a minute. Then they show you while you with the baby. You know, you can't talk to your family and boyfriend about different stuff like that. You can talk to the doula about being a mom and different stuff.... she know where I'm coming from and I know where she coming from and she helped me in that way, mother to mother.

Another mother shared the importance of understanding new parenting skills:

It was more like one-on-one, and it was like, more in depth, because the doulas really got down to the...nitty gritty, okay this is going to happen so you might as well deal with it. You know what I mean? They all tell us the sweet stories, but then again they'll let us know that there are, well not everything is perfect for the pregnancy and after...I probably would have been nuts without them... I'm not the same.... I feel different from when I first came here. I am a better parent. I feel mature or something, like I am doing, like I am a part of something here.

Encouraging breastfeeding. Participants reported that doulas emphasized characteristics of good infant health and encouragement of breastfeeding. Doulas are trained and skilled to help promote early breastfeeding after birth. Home visiting assessments conducted by the doulas focus on breastfeeding success and challenges. One mother remembered:

> They asked me how much she was and was I breastfeeding.... Then after that (the doula) would call to see if I was okay, to see how the breastfeeding was going, because my milk didn't come out for until like the next day after I had my son. She was calling to make sure it was okay, so we kept in contact cause she breastfeed her kids.

Open Comments by Study Participants

All participants were provided an opportunity to respond to the question: "Are there other comments you would like to share related to your social support, experience with the doula, or hope for your future?"

Two themes emerged from participants: uncertainty about the future, and recognition of the need for continued assistance. One participant said:

> Teens should participate in this program, and one thing that lets you know that they care is every time you come they ask, "Do you need anything?" or "Are you okay, is everything in your house okay?" You don't hear that in most programs, they just start the talk.

All of those responding described the importance and strong value that they felt personally for the community agency and doula program.

> Well I don't really see any difference in being a young mother than a mother, but I want to convey this about the doula program, its like, if you don't have anybody this can be your somebody here, and they can teach

you a lot. You might not have anybody to turn to, some people don't have
a mother in their lives, or their father ran out on them or something, but
they give you hope and help you plan your future and stuff.

Conclusions

Participants identified the community-based doulas and the community agency's
teen program as their primary network of social support and assistance. The program provided both tangible and nontangible resources. Notable value was
placed on the nature of the extended relationship with the doula. Although published studies traditionally define doula in terms of care being rendered during
labor and delivery (Gagnon Waghorn, & Covell, 1997; Hodnett & Osborne,
1999; Hofmeyr et al., 1991; Kennell, Klaus, McGrath, Robertson, & Hinkley,
1991; Klaus & Kennell, 1997; Klaus, Kennell, Robertson, & Sosa, 1986; Scott,
Berkowitz, & Klaus, 1999; Sosa, Kennell, Klaus, Robertson, & Urrutia, 1980;
Zhang, Bernasko, Leybovich, Fahs, & Hatch, 1997), in this setting, the community-based doula supported women during pregnancy, labor and delivery, and
early parenting.

Findings from this study suggested that the doulas provide unique types of support: nonjudgmental caring, continuous support at the hospital bedside, and
encouragement toward a brighter future. This support often exceeded described
support from primary family members. This may be explained partially by the
fact that many of the participants did not have substantive family support or had
negative support. The community doulas frequently became replacement author-
ity figures. The doulas' life experiences within the neighborhood, when combined
with their knowledge, skill, and training in doula work, facilitated formation of
a special, personal relationship. Doulas provide information on sensitive topics
that the teens cannot easily discuss with family members. They respect the teen's
ability to make informed decisions and share frank discussions on the harshness
of life in their neighborhood to provide motivation toward a better future.

Results from this qualitative study support earlier findings in adult populations in that the presence of a doula enhances a new mother's feeling of emotional support and care during labor, provides modeling of responsive interaction with her newborn infant, and increases the mother's self-confidence. Doula care during the prenatal period provides an additional early opportunity to establish trust and caring as well to prepare the teen for labor and delivery. The doula's involvement in supporting participants through labor and delivery was recognized as significant and meaningful. Participants appreciated the doulas' modeling infant care through home visiting, teaching parenting skills, enhancing maternal competence, and providing breastfeeding support. Doula care postdelivery also provides an opportunity for ongoing assessment of the new mother and baby by a trusted caregiver.

The extended relationship promotes personalization of care from the doula and establishes a bond with the teen. Some participants said that they would never forget the care and personal attention they received during labor. Many reported having no other adult with them in labor other than their doula. This intimate caring certainly provided opportunities for a cementing, or reciprocal bonding, of the relationship between the doula and the mother; that relationship, magnified during labor and birth, may assist in modeling the formation of attachment behaviors (doula to laboring mother, mother to newborn baby). Klaus et al. (1986) and Klaus and Kennell (1997) suggested that constant human support by experienced doulas positively affected obstetrical and neonatal outcomes in adult populations and that doula-supported women also reported a greater self-esteem and higher regard for their baby.

Participant responses suggested that there are differences between doula support and other kinds of health care provider support. A significant theme was the doula's style of providing education in a manner that was responsive to the mother's specific needs. Support was described as relational and caring: sisterlike, woman to woman, mother to daughter, or friend to friend. Findings from this study suggest that doulas possess attributes that were highly valued, unique, and supportive.

Follow-Up Focus Session: 3 Years Later

In the fall of 2004, 7 of the original study participants volunteered to be re-interviewed in a focus group session to talk about their lives since participating in the community-based doula program 3 years earlier. The purpose of this discussion was to encourage reflective comments about their experiences with the doula program, to ask about the doulas' effect on their lives, and to explore whether the program enhanced their ability to become effective parents.

As many as possible of the original 30 participants were contacted. They were invited to return to the community center to meet the researcher and asked to participate in a group session to share their birth and parenting stories (Breedlove, 2004). Seven women, including 4 mothers with their children in tow, arrived eager to share their stories about experiences with the doula program. After individually giving voluntary consent, the women graciously gave their time by participating in a 3-hour, audiotaped focus group discussion. Each participant praised the community-based doula model while describing her own new role as an emerging mentor to the younger girls and children living in the neighborhood.

This follow-up discussion provided validation of identified themes from the 2001 study that suggested that doulas enhance maternal growth. All participants described themselves as good mothers to their children, stronger mothers compared with their peers who had less support. They embraced the idea of tenacity despite adversity. One of the returning mothers shared informally before beginning the guided discussion:

> The doulas say you have to take on [embrace], yeah embrace difficulty and not let the hardships overwhelm you. The doulas helped and are still here to make sure you learn, grow, and become better.

Participation in the Program

Participants were asked to reflect on why they chose to participate in the program; what they remembered as valuable experiences from the supportive care;

and whether the doulas influenced their choices during pregnancy, childbirth, and parenting.

One mother said that her extended family encouraged her to enroll, as they knew the services would help prepare her for childbirth and becoming a mom:

> My sister brought me up here. I was, like, I ain't going to that dang place....
> I ain't going to tell anybody my business, just so they can help me.... Then
> one day I just came over here and saw how the doulas were, who they were,
> and what it was like. And I was, like, okay, I would just try it. I was preg-
> nant and you want to know about all you can. Now I tell anybody that will
> listen about this place.

Valuing Doula Support

Themes that emerged from the original study were revalidated with similar frequency and significance by the returning mothers. They valued the doula care.
This included providing information regarding pregnancy, birth, breastfeeding,
and parenting; labor support; home visiting; infant education at home visits; provision of needed tangible items for the newborn; less formal yet stronger personal relationship than with other providers; and investment in the future of the
mother and her child.

One mother recalled many benefits from her doula:

> I learned that you could talk to your baby. I was, like, I ain't going to talk
> to my stomach; you know ... ain't no way I'm going to sit here and talk to
> my stomach. But the doula was just, like, she got something that she put
> on your ears and put on your stomach to make you hear the baby. I'm like
> okay, what is this baby doin', why am I hearing this, you know? I thought
> these people are crazy.... They were, like, talk to the baby, read a book to
> the baby, and I'm like what baby? It ain't even out yet. Well we just kept
> doing that every Tuesday, sit in a room. And I just started doing it and thought

115

it was interesting. Then the exercises they make you do before having the baby to keep the head down and to help with my back.

When I was in labor they calmed me down, rubbed my back, it was real good 'cause nobody was there but them. They would get ice then say something to make you laugh, so that was kind of cool. The whole time, like up to 13 hours, they would take turns to go get something to eat, but wouldn't eat in front of me. After it was all over they came to my house with big ol' gifts and stuff. First they talked to me about the baby, she had like an outline she followed, they talked a lot about the baby and took videotape of me with my baby. They also talked to me about the depression stages and ask me how I feel. They opened up conversation, you got a problem, you can call any of them.

A second mother shared:

If it wasn't for the doulas, a whole bunch of teen moms would be stuck with nowhere to go. They teach you the stuff you need to know.

All mothers remembered the significance of labor support and suggested that without the doula, they would have either had no support or less helpful support from family or friends. They appreciated the ability of the doula to provide constant bedside support including massage, options for relaxation, encouragement of non-medicated birth, and support for their choices.

Each mother highlighted the importance of the educational component, both pregnancy class and parenting classes conducted in a series format. Many reported learning more from the doulas than their prenatal health care providers. Topics included healthy nutrition in pregnancy, exercise, stress reduction, creation of birth plans, and preparation for breastfeeding. All mothers agreed that the group format of class with a doula facilitating was important. This provided an opportunity not only to learn from other young mothers and to talk about what was important at the time but also to hear from women within their community who had been through pregnancy and parenting before. Additionally, they reported that it was easier to ask questions in this setting, and they did not feel like they were alone in life when they were surrounded by other young mothers in a similar situation.

Tangible items of necessity for the baby were given through baby showers for the participants and gifts brought to new mothers at their first home visit after birth. Gifts included diapers, clothing, car seats, and infant home safety items. Home visits by the doulas were remembered as very positive. One mother described her home visit:

> They videotaped me feeding my baby…they made a copy and gave it to me. They showed the great things you were doing and how you talk and hold the baby, playing with them. They show you all the things the baby is doing, and what level they should be on and what things to work on and stuff like that. So they test them, I think like every time they age…like every few months I think.

Orientation to the Future

When asked to reflect on how they are today, compared with 3 years prior, all women echoed their belief that they were better mothers because of the doula program. One mother shared:

> They worked as a team, but one was different from anybody else…. She helped my baby's father and helped me a lot at the hospital. After I had my baby, in the delivery, she asked me to breastfeed, and I didn't, 'cause I didn't want the baby suckin' on me. But the second time she asked in the hospital she convinced me, and I breastfed my baby for 4 months. My momma wouldn't have let me breastfeed, but the doula helped me learn. I ain't never thought about breastfeeding until then… it makes you grow, it feels good to make your own decision…. Now I'm just going back to school, not only for myself but for my kids. The doula and them [center staff]

said, "Go back and get your GED and you will feel better when you get your GED." I actually went back to school and got my certificate, and I felt real good. And I was like, I did it! I'm in the job club now.

Another participant shared about her transition from uncertainty as an expecting mother to confidence and self-esteem as a mother:

Having a baby makes you grow up and they taught us to speak up. Like I was shy or whatever but, you know, they taught me how to speak up, if somebody doing something to your baby or anything you know. If it was just you, alone, you probably be like, I just let it go, don't care, but if it's harming your baby or whatever, now you gonna say something and speak up. You be like finding that voice we talking about. I'm stronger.

Like breastfeeding decision we talking about and stuff like that. For me, when I was younger and pregnant, I was, like, that makes your breasts sag, but my baby was sick when he was born. He was 2 weeks early, and it was like they said, I had to breastfeed him anyway to help him. I am a strong advocate for breastfeeding.... But you know, if I didn't know that from the doulas, I wouldn't know you got to learn to put your baby first.... Now I tell everyone.

Another mother offered her thoughts about becoming a stronger and more confident mother:

They really taught me how to treat a newborn. Cause, I was young, and my momma, she wasn't there for me. They actually taught you how to deal with the baby. They taught you what to do, like they would actually get a doll and show you. It don't get no better than that. They taught me to care. They taught me to actually care for the baby.

When exploring comments on where these women were today related to their hopes and aspirations, and whether the doula program influenced their current situation in life, they quickly offered comments that suggested similar themes: being happier in life, more awareness of resources for assistance when needed, and a continued sense of a strong support and caring from the doulas and center staff:

> I've got some friends now. I've got somebody when I'm in pain to call and talk to. They're supportive and are willing to go through whatever I am going through with me. I'm older now, and I'm not in the program any more. They kicked me out when I was 21, but they're still willing to help out. It was a blessing; they're good people, helpful, and are now like my second mom. I changed a lot. I don't go out a lot anymore like I used to. I stay at home and take care of my kids.

Another mother shared:

> When I came here I wasn't responsible, because my mom ain't no good. I don't want to even get into that or I'll get cryin'. If you get raised like that, basically that is how you turn out. I came here, they gave me a whole turn around. I feel like I'm the best mom in the world…. They are who taught me how to be a momma. That's what they did. Be responsible, do something with your life, never give up. Just because you're 15 and have a baby don't mean it's the end of your life. That's what they taught me, and I am a good mom because of that.

Still another said:

> The doulas give lots of affection; in labor some people ain't got any support, like I couldn't even find my mother when I went into labor. You got to go look for her, somebody has to go find my momma instead of actually being there. When you in labor she [doula] show you all types of affection. When you be walkin', she be huggin' you. I think in the 9 months you and the doulas get a bond together. They taught you how to love. When I had my baby I was crying and actually askin' myself, "Why you cryin'?"

> because it was so unbelievable looking around. I'm looking at her [the doula]. I'm like, I just got to know this lady and she's like my buddy and my friend. She's sitting there holding my hand, and I be thinking "where the heck is my parents?" That's when my emotions came down and I cried and cried...my momma doesn't know how.

The participants expressed strong belief that the community-based doulas were willing to talk about any subject without accusation or judgment; to listen first, always, before talking; and to be available always for assistance. Their comments described numerous situations in the traditional health care/social services model in which providers did not understand their social circumstances—could neither relate to them and how they think, nor establish a close bond of compassionate caring. They also experienced the doula and community center staff dedication to prioritizing individual needs while collectively caring for many. A closing comment by a returning mother captures the essence of this program:

> I just feel like they inspire you to do more. I can be like, so lazy, and I'm like, I knew how to do a lot of stuff, but I don't always know which way to go and they're, like, you've just got to do something! Do something! They call you at your house and see if you've filled out your college application. They say is your financial aid forms filled out yet? They got my cell phone and my house phone, and make sure you do what you got to do. I want to be a doula. I know I can help other young girls. Now we're saying to our friends, "You can talk to me girl!"

Conclusions

These mothers convincingly described the importance of the doulas' presence throughout their pregnancies and beyond. The doulas provided extraordinary mentoring during a brief window of time in the mothers' lives. Much remains to be discovered about the psychological implications of the community-based doula intervention. Significant components that set the community-based doula model apart from other interventions include the following:

- Doulas are women of the same culture, language, and neighborhood as their clients.

- Doulas provide ongoing relationship-based care.

- Doulas are available and present whenever they are needed.

- Doulas are invested in the future.

- Doulas provide assistance in pathways to success.

- Doulas accept where the teen is in life.

These qualities of support capture the essence of Dana Raphael's concept of mothering the mother.

It is not surprising that, without adequate nurturing throughout childhood, one has few skills to rely on in becoming a new mother. Such is evident by the many stories the young mothers shared. The community-based doula model provides a framework of support that assures an experienced adult companion will assist new mothers through a journey that is often overwhelming. Through this long-term, personal, and intimate relationship, a bond between doula and mother is developed and reflected in the relationship between the mother and her new child. As we reflect on the voices of these mothers whose lives were deeply influenced, we are impressed by the significant themes they shared about "their" community-based doula—the importance of continued presence, the ability to provide encouragement through caring, and the precious gift of unconditional "motherly" love.

References

Breedlove, G. K. (2001). *A description of social support and hope in pregnant and parenting teens receiving care from a doula.* Doctoral dissertation, University of Missouri—Kansas City. (UMI No. 3043597).

Breedlove, G. K. (2004). [Follow-up focus group of teens who received care from a doula]. Unpublished raw data.

Breedlove, G. K. (2005). Perception of social support from pregnant and parenting teens using community-based doulas. *The Journal of Perinatal Education, 14,* 15–22.

Gagnon, A., Waghorn, K., & Covell, C. (1997). A randomized trial of one-to-one nurse support of women in labor. *Birth, 24,* 71–77.

Hemminki, E., Virta, A., Koponen, P., Malin, M., Kojo-Austin, H., & Tuimala, R. (1990). A trial on continuous human support during labor: Feasibility, intervention and mother's satisfaction. *Journal of Psychosomatic Obstetrics and Gynecology, 11,* 239–250.

Hodnett, E. D., & Osborn, R. (1989). A randomized trial of the effects of monitrice support during labor: Mother's views two to four weeks postpartum. *Birth, 16*(4), 177–183.

Hofmeyr, G., Nikodem, V., Wolman, W., Chalmers, B., & Kramer, T. (1991). Companionship to modify the clinical birth environment: Effects on progress and perceptions of labour, and breastfeeding. *British Journal of Obstetrics and Gynaecology, 98,* 756–764.

Orenstein, G. (1998). A birth intervention: The therapeutic effects of doula support versus lamaze preparation on first-time mothers' working models of caregiving. *Alternative Therapies, 4,* 73–81.

Kennell, J., Klaus, M., McGrath, S., Robertson, S., & Hinkley, C. (1991). Continuous emotional support during labor in a U.S. hospital. *Journal of American Medical Association, 265,* 2197–2201.

Klaus, M., & Kennell, J. (1997). The doula: An essential ingredient of childbirth rediscovered. *Acta Paediatrica, 86,* 1034–1036.

Klaus, M., Kennell, J., Robertson, S., & Sosa, R. (1986). Effects of social support during parturition on maternal and infant morbidity. *British Medical Journal, 293,* 585–587.

Scott, K., Berkowitz, G., & Klaus, M. (1999). A comparison of intermittent and continuous support during labor: A meta-analysis. *American Journal Obstetrics and Gynecology, 180,* 1054–1059.

Sosa, R., Kennell, J., Klaus, M., Robertson, S., & Urrutia, J. (1980). The effect of a supportive companion on perinatal problems: Length of labor, and mother–infant interaction. *The New England Journal of Medicine, 11,* 597–600.

Zhang, J., Bernasko, J. W., Leybovich, E., Fahs, M., & Hatch, M. C. (1997). Continuous labor support from labor attendant for primiparous women: A meta-analysis. *Obstetrics and Gynecology, 88*(4), 739–744.

Chapter 8

Replication of the Chicago Health Connection Model

I t has been 10 years since Chicago Health Connection (CHC) initiated the Chicago Doula Project and 5 years since we began to work with the first replication site. The first 5 years of work concretized the community-based doula model, validated its effectiveness in a low-income teen population, and brought national attention to the possibilities of this work. The second 5 years resulted in the development of replication sites across the state of Illinois and in seven other states. The diverse agencies that have engaged in replication and the varied communities served by their programs testify to the wide applicability of the model. The diversity of local settings also has challenged us to find an approach to replication that is both flexible and faithful to the model.

CHC is actively involved in outreach to new communities and in partnerships with new and developing replication sites. We have built a team of staff and consultant replication trainers that includes nurses, community health workers (CHWs), and community-based doulas and advocates, and CHC coordinates a network of existing and emerging community-based doula programs around the country.

This chapter focuses on the practicalities of replicating CHC's community-based doula model.

A Replication Story

The Southeast Heights neighborhood of Albuquerque, New Mexico, is home to a mixture of populations, including a large proportion of Mexican, Cuban, and Vietnamese immigrants and refugees. Southeast Heights contains one of the highest concentrations of limited-English-speaking (LES) residents in the city (Gorsline-Flamm, 2002). A survey conducted by the Women, Infants, and Children (WIC) program in 1998–1999 showed that only 4% of Vietnamese women in Albuquerque were breastfeeding their babies, a rate similar to that of other immigrant and refugee women who leave traditional cultures to come to North America. A small group of public health advocates conducted a community health assessment in early 1999 to explore the issues around maternal and child health for LES Vietnamese and Latina women in the area. Initially, they were interested in finding an innovative approach to increasing breastfeeding rates, but community residents and health providers in the focus groups identified a broader set of issues.

Women described being terrified during childbirth because they couldn't understand their caregivers. Providers confirmed that language barriers prevented LES women from getting the care they needed for themselves and their children. All participants identified the need for culturally appropriate health information and support during pregnancy, birth, and the first postpartum months. An active—and very vocal—committee of community residents who had been interviewed for the assessment met to discuss the issue. This collaborative group began to consider a program that trained bilingual community women to be both doulas and medical interpreters. A graduate student activist applied for a grant from the W. K. Kellogg Foundation to develop a doula project to serve Vietnamese and Hispanic families in Southeast Heights. In 1999, the Support, Empowerment, Advocacy and Doulas (SEAD) Project was formed.

It took more than 18 months for the project advisory committee to define its objectives, find additional funding, and bring essential stakeholders to the table, including the New Mexico Department of Health, the University of New Mexico, local doulas, and community groups. One of the project directors was a pediatrician who had worked with Chicago Health Connection in Chicago and recommended a partnership with CHC. The new project looked first at local doulas to help develop the program but ultimately decided that the community-based model developed in Chicago was a better match. This model served the local needs identified by the community and, in addition, provided much needed education and jobs to community members, validated women's work on behalf of their communities, and valued the diversity of Southeast Heights. In the fall of 2000, CHC conducted two site visits, one to facilitate a number of stakeholders' meetings, and a second 2-day training of trainers for the SEAD Project. SEAD doulas began serving women in Southeast Heights in June of 2001, and the first doula-attended births were celebrated in July.

The SEAD Project was similar to the Chicago Doula Project in its essential components but was developed in response to specific community needs in Albuquerque. The project served Vietnamese women and Latinas, a population that was of mixed age and income level but was self-defined as underserved. The doulas were trained with CHC's community-based doula curriculum but were also trained as medical interpreters. Strengths and challenges of the project were both similar to and different from those of the Chicago project. Since the initial phone conversation in February 1999, CHC has continued a complex and mutually beneficial partnership with SEAD.

Seeds of Change

Starting a new program, as with the SEAD Project, begins with motivation. Change takes energy, and energy comes from a process that moves people from individual experience to common vision.

We believe that the movement toward action, both for individuals and communities, begins with internal personal issues. We begin moving communities toward action by creating opportunities for individuals to talk in groups about their own experiences, to share their own narrative of individual and then communal experiences around childbirth and family development. The sharing of personal experience in a group and the discussion of common themes lead to a broader vision of the reality of people's lives in a local community. An identification of need and an assessment of community resources are necessary first steps for replicating the community-based doula model. This is a process that depends on collaboration and community involvement. CHC trainers and consultants work closely with local collaborators to develop a program tailored to the unique needs and strengths of the community.

Essential Components of the Community-Based Doula Model

Replication of our community-based doula model develops within a framework of essential components. We do not use a one-size-fits-all structure. Local replications are developed locally to respond to local needs and circumstances but always within the framework of essential model components. Local decisions include defining the community being served and deciding how long doulas see families, how doula services are integrated into existing family support, and so forth.

Because the positive outcomes of community-base doula support are generated from a clearly defined program, fidelity to the core model is necessary to replicate those outcomes. These essential components, described more fully in chapter 3, include:

- Doulas are paid staff recruited and hired from the community being served.

- Participating families have extended involvement with doulas.

- Extensive training, ongoing reflective supervision, peer support, and administrative support are priority components of successful programs.

- Collaborative community partnerships are necessary to provide continuity of care to families.

- Communities use a logic model to define desired perinatal health and parent–infant relationship outcomes.

Stages of Program Replication

The formal replication process begins with submission of an application form to CHC. We developed the application questions to stimulate local conversation and self-assessment. Additionally, the questions provide a test of organizational capacity and readiness to make a commitment to doula program development.

Once we engage with an agency, a group of organizations, or a community, CHC facilitates a gathering of stakeholders. Building a consensus on community need and priority issues is necessary for broad commitment and buy-in.

Who are the potential stakeholders? They may be clinics, hospitals, human service agencies, individual health or social service providers, community residents and activists, government and civic leaders, and potential funders. It is important to identify what programs exist in the local community to serve families and include them in the planning.

What are other community assets? Some communities may have a history of activism around family issues. Others may have developed collaborative structures to address community problems.

How can available resources—both human and financial—be engaged in developing a strong new program? This stage of the process involves a considerable amount of conversation. Its forward movement depends on bringing all the stakeholders to the table, asking the right questions, and listening carefully to the evolving answers.

The development of a broad-based collaboration involves clear, multidirectional communications, trust-building, and a mutually acceptable decision-making process. When there are enough invested stakeholders and a sense of common vision, there can be a commitment to action. This threshold may be reached before or after the necessary resources, both human and capital, are identified.

The next step is creating an action plan for the development of the local doula project. The plan is tailored to the specific assets and needs of the community. Before making decisions about lead agencies, venues for providing services, and medical partners, it is essential to understand who will be best served by the program, where families access services, what geographic or political barriers might affect access, and what resources already exist to support programs. It is useful to integrate the community-based doula program into existing family support services.

A project workgroup, steering committee, or similarly named action group should bring representation of stakeholders, including community residents, to decisions made about the project. The steering committee moves the process forward, with regular feedback and consultation from a broader group of stakeholders. Some groups may find it challenging to reach a balance between agency representatives and community residents, but such an effort makes it more likely that decisions will represent both community concerns and agency goals and include the strengths and resources of both perspectives (Sierra Health Foundation, 2004).

It is helpful to use a theory of change model (Diehl, 2002) to identify priority outcomes, key program elements, and strategies to achieve those conditions. This can be stated as a logic model, a document that specifies program goals, services, indicators of success, and the rationale for the effect (Yarbrough, 2003). It is also helpful to hold at least one open community meeting to explain the doula program to potential program allies and to get feedback on program issues before proceeding further in the replication process.

As the funding for the project is developed and the program design clarified, training of trainers and administrators begins. For our replication sites, CHC conducts an intensive 2-day session that describes the popular education training approach. The doula training curriculum is presented, and participants practice delivering sections of the curriculum to each other. The principles of the project and the core values are described, modeled, and practiced. Training is tailored to the specific conditions of the community. The strategy of training a team of local trainers is a community development approach. It builds a cadre of people who are skilled and capable of keeping the project going.

Sustainability and evaluation are two sides of the same coin. Sustainability depends on proving effect, which is why it is necessary to plan for evaluation from the beginning, including budgeting evaluation funds. A participatory approach to evaluation involves the community in defining priority questions and anticipated outcomes and incorporates regular testing and reevaluation of community needs, program process, and continued buy-in of stakeholders. This is assured by establishing an ongoing process and schedule of program review.

Organizational Criteria: What Does It Take to Start a Doula Program?

Community involvement is integral to the doula model. For our replication, CHC seeks organizations that are committed to understanding and responding to community needs. This is demonstrated by the agency's efforts in conducting a community needs assessment. We require agencies to have a clear planning process in place and to demonstrate program responsiveness and community involvement in their previous or existing programs. We evaluate examples of working collaborations in the community, including agreements and planning documents. Additionally, agencies are required to identify community representatives with whom they will collaborate on replicating and launching a doula program in their community.

When we do a site visit, we can tell that a collaboration truly represents stakeholder groups if we observe the following:

• The conversation has the comfort that comes from a history of mutual engagement,

- The participants in the room reflect the composition of the community being served, and

- The plan for replication incorporates multiple perspectives or points of view.

If the collaboration does not include representation of stakeholder groups and community residents, we encourage the group to identify who is not at the table and ways to draw them in.

Internal agency culture frequently affects the ultimate success of a doula program replication process. Organizations that devote regular time and effort to communicating with staff for support and guidance are more likely to be successful. Such agencies demonstrate a reflective supervision style and a nurturing environment that supports continued staff development and growth. In our experience, an organization with a team culture translates into staff members who show flexibility in program operations and adapt easily to new ideas and responsibilities.

New community-based doula programs are not necessarily easy to start. The process requires strong executive leadership and support. We have learned that agencies with strong communications and clear decision-making systems are better at launching a successful program. For our replication, we look for organizations that are fiscally sound, have a clear vision and mission, and can articulate how the doula program will help them achieve their vision and mission. We evaluate how the agency has managed change in the past and how it has planned, implemented, and sustained new program ideas.

Building a partnership around innovation requires integrating multiple agendas, overcoming turf issues, building trust among diverse stakeholders, and incorporating aspects of change into systems that may not have worked together previously. Every collaborative group has its own assets and weaknesses. Successful groups develop a common vision over time. They find a comfortable basis on which to learn from each other and are able to develop action plans and solutions that serve the needs of a broad constituency. This is an ongoing circular process that builds stakeholder investment over time, takes collective action, evaluates results and sustainability of solutions, revises and develops new systems, and continues the creative process.

Status of Community-Based Doula Program Replication

CHC works with approximately 27 community-based doula programs in eight states: Illinois, New Mexico, Georgia, Minnesota, Arizona, Colorado, Indiana and Washington. The agencies and the communities they serve are quite diverse. They include programs that serve young parents, communities whose members have limited English skills, and women in treatment for addiction. They focus services around child care centers, public schools, and community clinics. They have in common provision of family support services to communities that are self-defined as underserved. These may be families generally described as high risk or vulnerable—for example, teen parents, socially isolated families, and communities who face language barriers to accessing services or significant racial or ethnic health disparities.

CHC also coordinates a network of community-based doula programs, including our replication sites and agencies interested in or working to become formal replications sites. We gathered in Chicago for a national conference in 2002 and did so again in 2006. We collaborate on common issues, including evaluation of program process and outcomes and advocating for the development of sustainable funding for community-based doula programs.

Program Creation and Re-Creation: A Second Story

The Georgia Campaign for Adolescent Pregnancy Prevention (G-CAPP) collaborated with CHC to develop the second community-based doula replication site outside Illinois. G-CAPP began a formal collaboration with

CHC in 2001, and the Healthy Beginnings doula program began supporting pregnant and parenting teens in Atlanta in December 2002. The program was initially based in the Fulton County Health Department, a large institution unaccustomed to developing innovative, nontraditional programs. Two full-time doulas were hired and placed in two community-based organizations, one serving an African American neighborhood and one serving Spanish-speaking teens.

The program provided services for 2 years with strong program outcomes. After 2 years, however, Fulton County decided for administrative reasons not to renew the contract. As G-CAPP began to reassess the needs and resources of their local community, the executive director approached Families First, a highly regarded social service agency in Georgia, to provide a new home for the program. Families First was a good fit for this innovative approach to supporting pregnant and parenting teens. Healthy Beginnings now continues to grow as a program of Families First. They have hired a Spanish-speaking lead doula and two additional doulas as backup. The program is now in a phase of "re-creation," building new organizational relationships and program structures, and re-instituting consistent support for the original two doulas in a new site.

CHC has been involved in a consulting and support role at each stage of Healthy Beginnings' program development. We continue to engage in the reassessment of program process and outcomes, and in actively supporting the reflective process that is taking Best Beginnings to a new, stronger beginning.

This is a story of success, of a program that is responding creatively to challenging circumstances. G-CAPP's experience is a good example of the circular process of program development. Strong programs assess community needs and resources, develop responsive structures, recognize challenges and changing circumstances, reevaluate, and move toward new relationships and structures (See Figure A). A program that is fully committed to responding to community circumstances will have the ability to adapt to change. In the final analysis, the most important criterion for successful doula program development and sustainability is how strongly the community and the organization involved want the program to survive.

Figure A

Framework of Community-based
Doula Program Replication

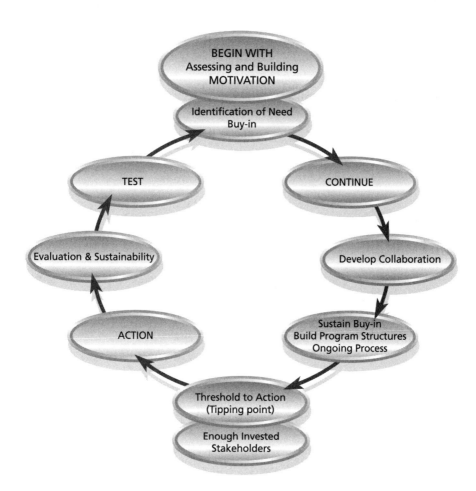

Program Replication/Expansion

Readers who are interested in assessing whether their agencies might be ready to develop a doula component may want to consider the following essential components and questions.

Organizational Criteria

What does it take to start a community-based doula program? Potential program replicators should consider carefully whether this model will be a good fit for local conditions and will address important community issues. The following are essential components of this model:

- Doulas are paid staff, recruited and hired from the community being served.

- Participating families have extended involvement with doulas.

- Extensive training, ongoing reflective supervision, peer support, and administrative support are priority components of successful programs.

- Collaborative community partnerships are necessary to provide continuity of care to families.

- Communities define desired perinatal health and parent–infant relationship outcomes, and develop and refine the program to attain those outcomes.

Self-Assessment

Self-assessment is the first step to program development. The following questions are intended to stimulate a process of local conversation that will begin the analysis leading to collaboration and decision.

- What is the community that will be served by this project?

  –What are its needs around birthing and support of young families?

  –What are the resources now in the community?

  –Who are the potential collaborators for this project?

  –How are community voices included in planning?

  –Is this project a priority for the community being served?

- What is the capacity of the core group to develop a sustainable new project?

  –Who are your allies?

  –How extensive and deep are your contacts?

  –What is the reputation of your organization within the community being served? Among other organizations? Among funders? Among public officials?

- What are your strengths and what are your deficits?

- What is your access to private and public funding?

- Are there individuals with dedicated time to organize a new project?

Collaborative Groups

Successful community-based doula program development depends on organizations or collaborative groups who:

- Have established and documented the need for the program,

- Have an understanding of or past experience working with lay people in a professional capacity (CHWs, lay health advisors, paraprofessional home visitors),

- Can devote the staff time of an organizational decision-maker to program development,

- Have a history of successful collaboration, and

- Have a history of incorporating innovative programs and managing organizational change.

New Partners

CHC continues to partner with new organizations interested in replicating the community-based doula model. If you are motivated and willing to commit the time, personnel, and resources needed to implement and sustain this program, we can be a partner in achieving your goals. As an organization with consistent and demonstrated results, CHC continues to refine and improve the replication process, ensuring the effect of this model—one connection at time.

References

Diehl, D. (2002). *Issues in family support evaluation: Report from a meeting of national thought leaders.* Chicago: Family Support America.

Gorsline-Flamm, E. (2002). Prenatal, labor and delivery support through doula-interpreters. *International Journal of Childbirth Education, 17*, 20–21.

Sierra Health Foundation. (2004). *A 10-year investment in community building to improve children's health: Evaluation of the Community Partnerships for Healthy Children Initiative.* Sacramento, CA: Author.

Yarbrough, K. (2003). Planning for success: Mapping goals, services, and outcomes for program improvement. *Birth to Five Project: Identifying and promoting best program practices, Issue No. 2.* Chicago: Ounce of Prevention Fund.

Chapter 9

Social Forces Affecting Community-Based Doula Practice

Community-based doula practice has developed within the social forces and historical context around the support of birthing families. Birth outcomes with doula support are, therefore, affected in complex ways by broad economic, social, and medical factors that profoundly influence the possibilities for positive, empowering birth experiences. Community-based doulas struggle with these challenges, as described in chapter 6. On a deeper level, the success of community-based doula programs may be limited by practices that interfere with some of the primary goals of such programs—normal vaginal and nontraumatic deliveries, successful breastfeeding, the development of responsive mother–infant interaction, and mothers' self-efficacy, or the belief in one's ability to master life events. This chapter examines some of these practices in the context of community-based doula practice

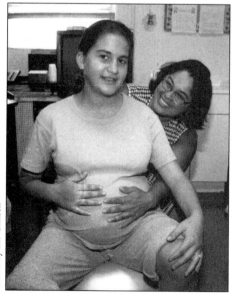

Photo by Liz Chilsen

The Medicalization of Childbirth

Medical practice around pregnancy, birth, and the early postpartum period affects the experience of mothers and babies and thus affects the involvement of parents and their children. Betsy Lozoff and her colleagues urge a re-examination of these practices in the groundbreaking 1977 article, "The Mother–Newborn Relationship: Limits of Adaptability." The authors argue that perinatal medical management has interfered with the beginnings of the mutual involvement of mothers and infants:

> The widespread disturbance in parenting and the fragmentation of families in the United States suggest the need for re-examination of those medical practices that affect the involvement of parents with their children. Throughout most of human history, anatomic, physiologic, and behavioral adaptations within the mother–infant relationship have been capable of providing the nutrition, protection, and social stimulation necessary for the infant's survival and development. Perinatal medical care was introduced in this century with the purpose of further decreasing mortality and morbidity by preventing infection and managing physical problems. There is now a growing body of evidence that these advances inadvertently alter the initiation of the mother–infant relationship and that some mother–infant pairs may be strained beyond limits of adaptability. (Lozoff, Brittenham, Trause, Kennell, & Klaus, 1977, p. 1)

Before the 20th century, childbirth took place in the home surrounded by close female relatives and friends. Birth was considered a natural, normal—although sometimes life-threatening—event. It was considered the exclusive province of women, with friends and family providing social support and midwives providing skilled attendance. This gathering of women at the bedside of the birthing mother has been called "social childbirth" (Wertz & Wertz, 1989). It was not until the Revolutionary War period that educated physicians began attending births at all, and it was not until the 1930s that medicine began to gain hegemony over the care of pregnant women (Wertz & Wertz, 1989). As the 20th century ended, 95% of all births in this country took place in the hospital. Birth has become a medical event, and birthing women have become "patients" (Jordan, 1993).

We are currently in an era of widespread and growing acceptance of the medical model of childbirth. Technological developments in the medicalization of childbirth have come with the initiation of institutional policies that can interfere with the natural human physiologic process. These include the following:

- Routine continuous electronic fetal monitoring with associated limitations of mothers' movement during labor,

- An increase in the universal use of intravenous fluids,

- Limiting the number of supportive individuals in labor and delivery areas,

- Encouraging narcotic and regional anesthesia—notably epidural anesthesia—for management of pain,

- Limiting alternative comfort measures or coping techniques in labor, and

- Transferring newborns to the nursery for immediate assessment after birth.

There has also been a recent and growing trend toward viewing elective cesarean section (choosing a cesarean section with no medical reason) as medically and socially acceptable. This has contributed to the rising rates of this procedure, which accounted for 29% of all births in the United States in 2004. A committee opinion in 2003 from the American College of Obstetricians and Gynecologists (ACOG) supported the ethical justification for elective cesarean delivery, also known as "patient choice cesarean" or "cesarean on demand" (ACOG, 2003).

Oxytocin

A growing body of research is investigating the effects of the medicalization of childbirth on the normal hormonal orchestration of late pregnancy and birth. These hormonal changes set the physiological stage for important interactions between mothers and their newborns, including breastfeeding and the formation of mother–infant attachment (Lothian, 2005). One hormone of fundamental importance is oxytocin, an ancient substance that is found in mammals of all species (Uvnas-Moberg & Francis, 2003). The use of common medical interventions affects oxytocin levels during and after birth, with possible consequences for both mother and infant, as oxytocin plays such an important role during this period. Elevated oxytocin levels stimulate milk ejection, and studies have established that newborns when placed in skin-to-skin contact with their mothers immediately after unmedicated birth exhibit behaviors that stimulate the release of maternal oxytocin in the first hour postpartum. These behaviors include stepping movements, or "crawling to the breast," locating the mother's breast without assistance, hand movements that massage the breast, and latching on to the breast and sucking (Matthiesen, Ransjo-Arvidson, Nissen, & Uvnas-Moberg, 2001; Uvnas-Moberg & Francis, 2003).

Oxytocin is important not only for breastfeeding and mother–infant attachment but also for the development of other social bonds bonds (Uvnas-Moberg & Francis, 2003). Research published in 2005 in the *Proceedings of the National Academy of Sciences* (Wismer Fries, Ziegler, Kurian, Jacoris, & Pollak, 2005) raised provocative questions about the hormonal basis of the mother–child bond and early social experience. Researchers studied oxytocin levels in two groups of 4-year-old children: one group who had spent their infancies in orphanages in Romania and Russia with a lack of emotional care and were later adopted into families in the United States and the other group who were raised with their biological families. Unlike the latter group of children, whose oxytocin levels were found to rise after a half hour of physical interaction with their mothers, the adopted children did not have increased levels of oxytocin.

Research on the foundational importance of oxytocin on the formation of social bonds and on breastfeeding raises intriguing questions about the birth experience and the possible effects of common medical practices and interventions on the hormonal milieu after birth.

Epidurals and Pain in Labor

Just as ACOG supports elective cesarean section, it also strongly supports medical management of labor pain, which contributes to the automatic assumption by medical professionals that birthing women all will want epidural analgesia.

In a joint statement, ACOG and the American Society of Anesthesiologists artic-
ulated this position:

> Labor results in severe pain for many women. There is no other circumstance
> in which it is considered acceptable for a person to experience untreated
> severe pain, amenable to safe intervention, while under a physician's care.
> (ACOG, 2000, p. 1)

The use of epidural analgesia in childbirth, however, is a subject of considerable
controversy and passionate discussion. Proponents of more natural comfort
measures are concerned not only about its safety and potential effect on the progress
of birth and on outcomes for mothers and infants, but also about a more philo-
sophical issue—the meaning of the experience of childbirth in a woman's life.

William McCool, Jana Packman, and Arthur Zwerling (2004) described the debate
as follows:

> The popularity of epidural anesthesia in obstetrics could be due to its abil-
> ity to adapt to a wide variety of labor pain patterns, while meeting the
> woman's desire for analgesia with full participation, awareness, and mem-
> ory of the childbirth experience. However, its increasing popularity has also
> made this form of anesthesia the center of debate over the role of pain relief
> in labor, with opinions ranging from those who promote epidural admin-
> istration for all women in labor to those who fear that epidurals are con-
> tributing to an increasing lack of control of laboring women over their own
> bodies and the very process of giving birth that they are experiencing
> (p. 508).

The common assumption that labor pain is always a negative experience is challenged by systematic reviews and primary studies that describe the experiences
of over 45, 000 women by an editor of the Cochrane Collaboration's Pregnancy
and Childbirth Group. Dr. Hodnett found that four factors are associated con-
sistently with satisfaction with childbirth:

- The amount of support a woman receives from caregivers,

- The quality of her relationship with her caregivers,

- Her involvement with decision making, and

- Her personal expectations.

She writes:

> Caregivers frequently assume that optimum pain relief during labor and birth is very important to most laboring women, and that those who say they wish to avoid pharmacologic pain relief measures are either martyrs or misinformed. However, the results concerning the impact of pain and pain relief on childbirth satisfaction were consistent across a wide variety of circumstances— when epidural analgesia was common or rare, across a wide variety of study designs and methods, in a variety of countries, over almost 30 years. Pain and pain relief generally do not play major roles in satisfaction with the childbirth experience, unless expectations regarding either are unmet. (The Nature and Management of Labor Pain Symposium Steering Committee, 2002, p. S12)

The results of the Listening to Mothers Survey conducted by the Maternity Center Association (Declercq, Sakala, Corry, Applebaum, & Risher (2002) concurred with these findings.

Cultural Attitudes About Birthing Pain

Culturally learned values and attitudes influence a woman's perception of labor pain as well as her expression of it. For instance, one comparative analysis of American and Dutch women found that American women expected labor to be more painful and anticipated needing more medication (Jordan, 1993). Consistent with these expectations, only 16% of the American women received no pain medication, in comparison with 61% of the Dutch women. According to the researcher:

> ...the Dutch see birth as a natural process and are biased against any sort of interference... Dutch birth participants hold a deep-seated conviction that the woman's body knows best and that, given enough time, nature will take its course. (Jordan, 1993, p. 3)

Many advocates for natural childbirth are concerned that interventions are potentially harmful to the progress of labor and to mothers and infants. Pain in birth is considered normal and appropriate, "pain with a purpose," unlike pain that is otherwise and normally associated with danger or disease.

This view of childbirth as a normal physiological process and life event—or even as a sentinel experience for a woman—has come to be regarded in recent years as a rather quaint notion in the United States, and those who believe in drug-free childbirth as an accomplishment, resulting in a sense of empowerment and pride, are often viewed as hopelessly old-fashioned or idealistic. In fact, some professionals in the United States suggest that primary elective cesarean section is an acceptable choice to avoid the pain of labor, and that view is gaining acceptance.

Nancy Lowe (2002) described Chapman and Gavrin's work on pain and suffering, illuminating and challenging this perspective:

> They propose that exhilaration rather than suffering may be experienced in response to threat when individuals are confident that they can cope masterfully with the challenge... If a parturient [birthing mother] understands the origin of her pain, perceives the eventual birth as highly positive (hence pain as a "good" sign of progress toward a desired goal), and perceives labor and its pain as non-threatening life experiences to be mastered, she may experience great pain but not suffer. This is a critical but difficult concept for the clinician who, in the interest of "helping," cannot understand why some women choose to persevere and labor without analgesia in the

face of pain. For these women, great pain, a great sense of accomplishment, and great enjoyment may be coexisting and independent themes of the labor experience. Childbirth becomes a life experience to be mastered...and through accomplishment and mastery has the potential to enhance self-esteem. (p. S22)

Epidural Analgesia

Epidural analgesia is now commonplace—almost universal—at many hospitals. It has come to be regarded by some as a woman's (patient's) right. An editorial in *American Family Physician* critiques this position:

> Access to professional labor support is considered a luxury for patients in most U.S. hospitals, and lack of access to epidural analgesia may result in legal action. The issue of patient choice is being used as a pretext for increasing technologic intervention in the birth process. A past president of the ACOG called for the right of a patient to choose cesarean delivery in the absence of maternal or fetal indications, and the American Society of Anesthesiologists suggests closing smaller hospitals that are unable to support universal access to epidural analgesia. However, neither organization advocates a broader range of labor support and pain management options to promote patient choice. ...In many hospitals, American women may feel that epidural analgesia is the only real choice they have. (Leeman, Fontaine, King, Klein, & Ratcliffe, 2003, p. 1026).

Current trends toward nursing shortages also may play a role. Many nurses simply do not have the time to provide bedside labor support, and it may be more practical, and economically beneficial, for hospitals to have the laboring woman remain in bed with epidural analgesia for relief of pain rather than depend on comfort measures that must be implemented by a continuously present caregiver.

Epidural analgesia is highly effective and widely regarded as safe for both mothers and infants, and the concentration and doses of medications given with epidural analgesia have decreased in recent years. However, certain adverse effects do occur. Even when they do not occur, other interventions that typically accompany the use of epidurals (e.g., intravenous fluids, continuous fetal monitoring, confinement to bed, blood pressure monitoring, and use of medications to stimulate or augment labor) may interfere with the normal progression of labor.

When adverse effects do occur, some are mild or of brief duration and may not require treatment, whereas others may affect the course of labor and, indirectly, the infant. The most commonly experienced side effects of epidural analgesia include the following:

- Longer second stage of labor (the time during which the woman pushes to deliver her infant),

- The use of oxytocin to augment labor,

- The use of medication to stimulate uterine contractions,

- Fever,

- Instrumental delivery (e.g., vacuum extraction or forceps, which may result in increased lacerations and discomfort),

- Hypotension (low blood pressure),

- Increased urinary incontinence in the immediate postpartum period, and

- Pruritis (itching; Leighton & Halpern, 2002).

The common intrapartum fever experienced by mothers results in more frequent evaluation for infection and treatment with antibiotics, which may lead to an increased length of stay. This can result in increased costs of hospitalization, as well as separation of mother and infant, which can reduce opportunities to breastfeed and increase the likelihood of formula supplementation and, ultimately, breast-feeding failure.

Surveys indicate that women are not well informed about these potential side effects (Leeman et al., 2003). The Listening to Mothers Survey (Declercq, et al. 2002) indicates that women who express the desire for measures that will reduce or eliminate the pain of labor, including primary elective cesarean section, are dismayed to discover unanticipated postoperative pain.

A study of neurobehavioral outcomes in infants of mothers receiving epidurals in labor assessed newborns' behaviors on four occasions: 3 hours after birth and on Day 3, Day 7, and Day 28 postpartum (Sepkoski, Lester, Ostheimer, & Brazelton, 1992). The researchers found that infants in the epidural group had more disorganized motor behavior and orientation and were less alert than infants of mothers who did not have epidurals. They also found that mothers who had epidurals spent significantly less time with their infants in the hospital than mothers who did not have epidurals.

Epidurals and breastfeeding. In addition to possible side effects for the mother and baby, there are also some potentially adverse effects on breastfeeding. Researchers examined the effects of epidural anesthesia during labor on breast-feeding success and the use of formula supplementation with full-term healthy infants delivered vaginally (Baumgardner, Muehl, Fischer, & Pribbenow, 2003). The outcome studied was two successful breastfeeding experiences within 24 hours of delivery. A negative association was found between epidural anesthesia and breastfeeding success during this time, despite frequent attempts to breastfeed by these mothers. In addition, these infants were more likely to receive supple-mental bottles while in the hospital. The authors hypothesize that this difference may be attributable to the transient neuromotor impairment of the infant, which might affect breastfeeding skills.

It is widely acknowledged that early formula supplementation is deleterious to breastfeeding success and duration. Jan Riordan and her colleague (2000) studied infant feeding behavior in a prospective, blind, controlled study. The breast-feeding scores in the infants of unmedicated mothers were significantly higher than those whose mothers had epidurals. The authors noted:

> Although epidural medications are associated with suckling disorganization and weakness, these effects appear to be temporary and should not be a barrier to breastfeeding. It is possible that after a labor epidural, some mothers become discouraged when their baby does not breastfeed well (Riordan & Riordan, 2000, p. 9).

Delayed release of oxytocin for up to 36 to 48 hours may be another adverse effect of epidural analgesia, which may be significant, in light of the role of oxytocin in ensuring milk letdown and enhancing bonding of the mother to her infant (Ludington, 2001). Similarly, there is a significant decline in the release of oxytocin in response to the administration of morphine, commonly used postoperatively after cesarean section (Lindow, Hendricks, Nugent, Dunne, & Van der Spuy, 1999), and women who deliver by cesarean section have less release of oxytocin in connection with breastfeeding in the first 2 to 3 days after delivery, compared with women who have vaginal births (Uvnas-Moberg & Francis, 2003).

Pressure from health care providers. Many factors influence the likelihood of a laboring woman having an epidural, including the philosophy of the health care provider and the usual standards of care at each hospital. Doulas with clients cared for by nurse–midwives often report a striking contrast in options for nonpharmaceutical pain relief. When the laboring woman is permitted freedom of movement to ambulate, to labor in the shower or bathtub, or to sit on a birth ball, the doula has more ways to provide comfort measures to her client.

One situation frequently described by community-based doulas is pressure, to the point of coercion, by nurses and doctors to convince young mothers to have epidurals. A doula reports that one nurse was especially persistent in her efforts:

> My teen mom was very young but she knew what she wanted. She decided
> that she wanted to have natural childbirth. She didn't want an epidural. Well,
> her nurse asked her if she wanted the epidural, and my client told her "no."
> But the nurse kept asking, "Are you sure you don't want an epidural?" She
> told her that since her labor was being induced she would really need it.
> But still the girl told her that she didn't want—or need—an epidural. Well,
> that nurse actually told my client, "Betcha do." I could not believe it! And
> you know, she gave birth without that epidural after all. (Anonymous)

This kind of pressure can be hard to defend against, especially because laboring
women are quite suggestible to outside influences, particularly when labor is more
advanced. It is not unusual for a doula to report that "Do you want an epidural?"
is the very first question posed to their clients when the doctor or nurse enters
the room for the first time, sometimes even preceding an introduction. Many
doulas resent this manipulation of their vulnerable clients and would be more
accepting of the client's choice to have an epidural if indeed it was her own freely
made decision.

The Effect on Doula Care in Labor

The doula may find herself caught between her own bias toward the midwifery
model, which stresses the normality of most births, and the actual medical practices that are so common today. Feeling caught between her beliefs and her situation and having to negotiate her role can result in confusion and frustration
for the doula.

This trend toward increasing medicalization of care is also challenging to physicians. Current obstetrical care in the United States is being provided in a milieu
in which increasing numbers of obstetricians–gynecologists are leaving the practice of obstetrics. In many instances, this is a result of fear of being sued, which
according to a recent survey about medical liability conducted by ACOG is the
driving force behind the decision to stop delivering babies (ACOG, 2003).

Other changes in medical practice resulting from the fear of litigation include a decrease in the amount of high-risk obstetric care offered and an increase in routine medical interventions. Similarly, there is a trend to discontinue offering women the option of vaginal birth after cesarean, which also contributes to the growing rates of cesarean section.

Supporting Mastery and Competence

Increasingly in the United States, childbirth is viewed from a utilitarian perspective—primarily as a means to an end, with a focus on getting through childbirth with minimal pain, and as a process that requires active management and technological measures. In contrast, the doula operates in a nonclinical support role that uses low-tech, high-touch methods to support mothers in labor. Community-based doulas are trained to support their clients in making informed decisions about their health and health care and in advocating for themselves. For these practitioners, the process of labor has long-term implications. Consequently, they become protectors of women's birthing experiences.

The emotional effect of birth is both profound and enduring. Penny Simkin (2001) spoke about conversations with elderly women who recalled, with surprising detail, vivid memories of giving birth several decades earlier. In her interviews, certain themes emerged:

• Women whose birth experiences were positive reported enhanced feelings of self-esteem and self-confidence.

• Women who reported being involved in decision-making and who were treated well by nurses and doctors felt positively about their births.

• Women who recalled caregivers who said and did things the women did not want still expressed disappointment and even anger 15 to 20 years later.

Having a doula who believes in a mother's capacity to labor without epidurals, breastfeed her infant, and be a loving, good mother is empowering, and the mother becomes more capable of advocating for herself and her child. According to one doula:

> We help the girl have a voice. That goes back to empowerment. She feels like she's important. And she can do that for her baby. (Bonnie)

Advocating for a woman's opportunity to choose to experience natural childbirth is a core value of Chicago Health Connection and our doula program, and in today's environment, this is a controversial position—a vision of childbirth that is in tension with prevailing opinion. We believe that allowing and supporting birthing women to make good use of their biological, psychological, and social makeup to connect to their children and make the transition to parenthood is an essential choice. Choosing that experience and being successful is empowering. Supporting that choice nurtures competence.

Childbirth is a moment of risk and opportunity. Particularly for families who are vulnerable, for women who face huge challenges in their lives and have not had many chances to experience success, birth is a critical developmental opportunity for growth and change. The doula's support allows a woman who has been active in her own labor to process the meaning of her challenges, her triumphs, and her disappointments.

For some women, the opportunity to go through labor and delivery, to experience that ultimate challenge—with support, but summoning her own power—can be transformational. To hear a new mother talk about how proud she is of herself, how brave she was, to see the strength shining in her face, to watch how she holds her baby is to believe in the importance of this experience for the rest of her life, for all the ultimate challenges that she will face.

References

American College of Obstetricians and Gynecologists Committee Opinion (2000). Pain relief during labor. *Obstetrics and Gynecology, 95*(231), 1.

American College of Obstetricians and Gynecologists. (2003). *New ACOG opinion addresses elective Cesarean controversy.* Retrieved December 2, 2003, from http://acog.org/from_home/publications/press_releases/nr10-31-03-1.cfm

Baumgardner, D. J., Muehl, P., Fischer, M., & Pribbenow, B. (2003). Effect of labor epidural anesthesia on breastfeeding of healthy full-term newborns delivered vaginally. *Journal of the American Board of Family Practice, 16*, 7–13.

Declercq, E. R., Sakala, C., Corry, M. P., Applebaum, S., & Risher, P. (2002). Listening to mothers: Report of the first national U.S. survey of women's childbearing experiences. Executive summary. *Proceedings of Doulas of North America 9th International Conference, San Francisco, CA, July 24–27, 2002.*

Jordan, B. (1993). *Birth in four cultures: A Cross-cultural investigation of childbirth in Yucatan, Holland, Sweden and the United States.* Montreal, Quebec, Canada: Eden Press.

Leeman, L., Fontaine, P., King, V., Klein, M. C., & Ratcliffe, S. (2003, September 15). Management of labor pain: Promoting patient choice—Editorials. *American Family Physician, 68*, 1109–1112.

Leighton, B. L., & Halpern, S. H. (2002). The effects of epidural analgesia on labour, maternal, and neonatal outcomes: A systematic review. *American Journal of Obstetrics and Gynecology, 186*, 569–577.

Lindow, S. W., Hendricks, M. S., Nugent, F. A., Dunne, T. T., & Van der Spuy, Z. M. (1999). Morphine suppresses the oxytocin response in breast-feeding women. *Gynecologic and Obstetric Investigation, 48*(1), 33–37.

Lothian, J. A. (2005). The birth of a breastfeeding baby and mother. *The Journal of Perinatal Education, 14*(1), 42-45.

Lowe, N. K. (2002). The nature of labor pain. *American Journal of Obstetrics and Gynecology, 186*(Suppl.), S21–S22.

Lozoff, B., Brittenham, G. M., Trause, M. A., Kennell, J. H., & Klaus, M. H. (1977). The mother-newborn relationship: Limits of adaptability. *The Journal of Pediatrics, 91*(1), 1–12.

Ludington, S. (2001, December 5). *Kangaroo care for premature infants: State of the science and implications for clinical practice.* Presentation at Rush–Presbyterian St. Luke's Medical Center, Chicago, IL.

Matthiesen, A. S., Ransjo-Arvidson, A. B., Nissen, E., & Uvnas-Moberg, K. (2001). Postpartum maternal oxytocin release by newborns: Effects of infant hand massage and sucking. *Birth, 28*(1), 13–19.

McCool, W. F., Packman, J., & Zwerling, A. (2004). Obstetric anesthesia: Changes and choices. *Journal of Midwifery & Women's Health, 49*(6), 505–513.

The Nature and Management of Labor Pain Symposium Steering Committee. (2002). The nature and management of labor pain: Executive summary. *American Journal of Obstetrics and Gynecology. 186*(Suppl.), S1–S15.

Riordan, J., & Riordan, S. (2000). *The effect of labor epidurals on breastfeeding.* Park Ridge, IL: La Leche League International.

Sepkoski, C. M., Lester, B. M., Ostheimer, G. W., & Brazelton, T. B. (1992). The effects of maternal epidural anesthesia on neonatal behavior during the first month. *Developmental Medicine and Child Neurology, 34,* 1072–1080.

Simkin, P. (2001). *Remarks presented at the Doulas of North America (DONA) 7th International Conference,* Milwaukee, WI.

Uvnas-Moberg, K., & Francis, R. (2003). *The oxytocin factor: Tapping the hormone of calm, love and healing.* Cambridge, MA: DaCapo Press.

Wertz, R. W., & Wertz, D. C. (1989). *Lying-in: A history of childbirth in America, Expanded edition.* New Haven, CT: Yale University Press.

Wismer Fries, A. B., Ziegler, T. E., Kurian, J. R., Jacoris, S., & Pollak, S. D. (2005). Early experience in humans is associated with changes in neuropeptides critical for regulating social behavior. *Proceedings of the National Academy of Sciences, 102,* 17237–17240.

Chapter 10

Move to Action

All real learning is transformational. In the popular education model, training at the community level leads to individual and communal change—change in understanding, in skills, and in experience. Ultimately, the purpose of integrating these changes is to move to action.

Chicago Health Connection's (CHC's) work is based on this assumption. All of our training and program development facilitates the movement of participants to new ways of seeing their lives, new understanding of their capacities, and, we hope, to the decision to act.

We work with community-based organizations across the country who see the challenges facing families from up close. They tell us about high infant mortality rates, mental health problems and isolation, too many subsequent pregnancies among teens, young children not ready for school, the need to build bridges between the culture of families and the medical establishment, and the desire to maintain birth traditions in a highly medicalized health care environment.

Next-Step Goals

Across all of these challenges, CHC sees common goals:

• Improving infant health,

• Strengthening families, and

• Putting supports in place to ensure the ongoing success of families.

CHC's community–based doula program is a model that improves lives for families. We hope that this book has introduced the reader to the possibilities of the community-based doula model and provided some practical resources to facilitate development of similar programs.

Because birth is personal, the community-based doula model touches individuals and communities in a personal way. Engaging in discussion about the possibilities of this model can create excitement around organizing to better support birthing families in local communities and move stakeholders to action.

The potential represented by community-based doula practice challenges us to act on behalf of an expansion of this work. Action is necessary in three areas: program replication, evaluation, and advocacy for sustainable funding.

Program Expansion

This is a research-based model with demonstrated effect, and the possibilities of the model speak to diverse communities. Both the strong outcomes and the power of the work have generated excitement around the country, and CHC is working to help develop new replication sites in a variety of organizations. Our involvement includes outreach to interested communities, technical assistance on program development, and training (see chapter 8). The national network of existing and developing community-based doula replication sites is also beginning to engage in common work around data collection and advocacy.

Evaluation

Community-based doula work is 10 years old, and there is much to be learned about how practice is linked to positive outcomes. Critical next steps include collaborative work to examine the model in different settings, qualitative research to illuminate essential practice, standardization of data collection based on a logic model, and ultimately, randomized, controlled studies.

The force that drives program expansion is strong outcome data. We need to evaluate doula programs to document availability of the service—which demonstrates need for the programs—as well as to demonstrate its effect. Proof of effectiveness is increasingly necessary in today's funding environment. Therefore, evaluation becomes not just a way to describe and monitor program quality and effectiveness but is also an advocacy tool.

Advocacy

The greatest barrier to doula program expansion is a lack of funding in a contracting funding environment. Both the private and public sectors are taking a conservative funding stance, and it is increasingly challenging to develop innovative programs. The potential of this work will wither without creative and strategic advocacy and marketing of the outcomes of community-based doula programs.

CHC is engaging in advocacy on the national level in collaboration with our replication partners. Our efforts to market the model nationally have been enhanced by the screening and distribution of *A Doula Story* (Alpert, 2005), a powerful video documentary that follows the work of one community-based doula in Chicago and a number of the young women she serves.

The Case for Prevention and Early Intervention

Complicated problems need complex solutions. Successful community-based health promotion and prevention programs are high-touch and time-intensive models. To affect outcomes in high-risk families, we need to invest time and relationship building when it can make the most difference. This approach, however, challenges our current cultural and political preferences for short-term, high-tech, low-cost programs. The temptation in program development and replication is to implement a piece of a model, often the least expensive piece, and then to discredit the model when the implementation is not effective.

Community-based doula support results in improved outcomes for families when it is begun early in pregnancy; provided in an ongoing, intensive, relationship-based context; and implemented with attention to high-quality training and program support. It is an investment that prevents costly problems down the line. Truly, if we don't invest up front, we will pay the price later.

The marketing of limited hospital-based and fee-for-service doula models make the development of community-based doula programs more complicated. The trend toward decreased public funding for prevention services is an even greater challenge. It is increasingly difficult to develop and sustain public health or human service interventions whose benefits may lie well in the future. Making the case for prevention programs requires evaluation that considers cost-benefits as well as desired outcomes. Finding effective language and policy strategies to advocate for the community-based doula model is an essential task for the next decade. The real issue of sustainability for this model is the future of health care funding for community-based preventive and health promotional services.

"Make It So!"

Power is defined as "the capacity to produce a change" (Miller, 1991, p. 198). This powerful, nurturing model of support for birthing families can create profound change in individuals and in communities. We hope that the material in this book will stimulate you to go out and make it happen.

References

Alpert, D. (Director/Producer). (2005). *A doula story: On the front lines of teen pregnancy* [Documentary film]. Chicago, IL: The Kindling Group. (Available from The Kindling Group, 1222 West Wilson Avenue, Suite 2E, Chicago, IL 60640, www.adoulastory.org)

Miller, J. B. (1991). Women and power. In J. V. Jordan, A. G. Kaplan, J. B. Miller, I. P. Stiver, & J. L. Surrey (Eds.), *Women's growth in connection: Writings from the Stone Center* (pp. 197–205). New York: Guilford Press.

Appendix A

Findings From Studies of Labor Support

Study	Method	Participants	Interventions	Outcomes	Benefit Category
Sosa, Kennell, Klaus, Robertson, & Urrutia, 1980	Random assignment to control or experimental group.	40 healthy Guatemalan primigravida women randomized by drawing card, assigned 20 to usual care and experimental groups.	Control group had no support of family, friend, or continuous nurse per usual care hospital routines. Experimental group had constant doula support (untrained, friendly companion not met before).	Shorter labor for doula supported group; increased awake and interaction time with infant in mothers of experimental group including increased stroking of infant and talking to infant.	*Labor *Immediate psychological outcomes
Klaus, Kennell, Robertson, & Sosa, 1986	Random assignment to control or experimental group.	465 full term healthy primigravida women in early labor 3 cm or < with no medical problems on admission.	Control group followed usual care of hospital and did not receive consistent support. Women in the experimental group received supportive care from 1 of 3 lay Guatemalan women with no obstetric training.	Experimental group had significantly fewer complications including C-section and oxytocin augmentation and fewer admits of newborn to NICU. Of women with uncomplicated labor/birth with no interventions, those with doula support had a significantly shorter length of labor.	*Labor *Birth *Newborn

Continued on next page

Findings From Studies of Labor Support (cont'd)

Study	Method	Participants	Interventions	Outcomes	Benefit Category
Cogan & Spinnato, 1988	Random assignment to control or experimental group.	34 women at 26–37 weeks gestation (preterm) < 3 cm dilated on admission.	Control group had usual hospital routine care. Supported group had one-one labor support with Lamaze prepared childbirth educator who was also mother. Doulas received extra training and information about premature labor.	Support during labor was associated with reduction in abnormally long labor patterns, less frequent use of pain management in labor, and improved neonatal well-being as assessed by APGAR scoring.	*Labor *Birth *Newborn
Hodnett & Osborn, 1989	Random assignment to control or experimental group.	145 healthy primiparous women assigned to group in last trimester.	Control group had usual hospital care in Toronto Canada, intermittent presence of a nurse. Women in experimental group were assigned a monitrice that met with the woman twice in last trimester to discuss birth plans and provided continuous labor support.	Experimental group arrived at hospital significantly more advanced in labor and nearly twice as many had no medication during labor or birth. More had intact perineums. Mothers in the experimental group perceived receiving more comfort measures, emotional support, and advocacy from monitrice compared to control mothers who received intrapartum care by nurses; > 20% were lost to follow up on most outcomes.	*Labor *Birth *Immediate psychological outcome

Continued on next page

Findings From Studies of Labor Support (cont'd)

Study	Method	Participants	Interventions	Outcomes	Benefit Category
Kennell, Klaus, McGrath, Robertson, & Hinkley, 1991	Random assignment to control or supported group, and post randomization assignment to an observed group.	412 women ages 13–34, nulliparous, term, uncomplicated pregnancy admitted to hospital between 3–4 cm. Control n=204, Experimental n=212, Observed n=204.	Supported group received continuous support of a doula and the observed group was monitored by an inconspicuous observer.	Continuous labor support significantly reduced length of labor, rate of C-section and forceps birth. Use of epidural anesthesia was less by the supported group over the observed and control groups. Fewer infants born to mothers in supported group required prolonged hospital stay.	*Labor *Birth *Newborn
Hofmeyr, Nikodem, Wolman, Chalmers, & Kramer, 1991	Random assignment to control or experimental group.	189 nulliparous women without pregnancy complications, dilated < 6 cm on admission, with no supportive companion with them	Experimental group received support from 1 of 3 labor companions who stayed until the baby was born. Care was received the same in both groups otherwise. Usual care group received care from resident and nursing staff.	Companionship had no measurable effect on progress of labor. Use of analgesia was significantly reduced by supported group. Support group more likely to report they had coped well and their mean pain and state anxiety scores were lower than the control group. At 6 weeks postpartum, support group was more likely to be breastfeeding exclusively and to be feeding at flexible intervals.	*Labor *Birth *Newborn *Immediate psychological outcomes *Longer maternal/infant outcomes

Continued on next page

Findings From Studies of Labor Support (cont'd)

Study	Method	Participants	Interventions	Outcomes	Benefit Category
Gagnon, Waghorn, & Covell, 1997	Random assignment to control or experimental group.	413 nulliparous women > 37 weeks gestation admitted in labor.	Experimental group received one-one care from nurse. Usual care consisted of care from nurse for 2 to 3 laboring women with various types of supportive activities. Nurses took meal breaks and brief rest breaks. Participants had been admitted to the unit for an average of five hours prior to randomization. 36 women in the experimental group and 41 in the control group had epidural analgesia prior to randomization. 55 women in the experimental group and 45 in the control group had intravenous oxytocin augmentation of labor prior to randomization.	Supported group had 17% reduction in oxytocin augmentation. No differences found in other labor, birth, or newborn outcomes.	*Labor *Birth *Newborn

Continued on next page

Findings From Studies of Labor Support (cont'd)

Study	Method	Participants	Interventions	Outcomes	Benefit Category
Campero, Garcia, Diaz, Ortiz, Reynoso, & Langer, 1998	Qualitative study in Mexico City	Sixteen in-depth interviews post delivery determined satisfactory for findings using the Glaser and Strauss saturation framework	8 women had been accompanied by a doula and 8 had received usual hospital routine.	Women accompanied by doulas had a more positive childbirth experience. Differences between both groups related to their perceptions of the experience; treatment received from staff; information given and understanding; perception of routines; feelings about birth; and spatial and temporal perceptions.	*Immediate psychological outcomes
Langer, Campero, Garcia, & Reynoso, 1998	Randomized controlled trial	724 women admitted for delivery at a large social security hospital in Mexico City	Continuous support from one of ten women who had received doula training (six were retired nurses). Women in the comparison group received "routine care."	The frequency of exclusive breast-feeding 1 month after birth was significantly higher in the supported group; the duration of labor was shorter, and significantly more women perceived a high level of control over labor.	*Labor *Newborn *Immediate psychological outcomes *Longer maternal/infant outcomes

Continued on next page

Findings From Studies of Labor Support (cont'd)

Study	Method	Participants	Interventions	Outcomes	Benefit Category
Scott, Berkowitz, & Klaus, 1999	Meta-analysis of 11 clinical trials related to labor and birth outcomes	Support was provided by midwives and lay women. Laboring women were in good health and near or at term in all studies	Contrasted the influence of intermittent and continuous support provided by doulas during labor and delivery on five outcomes.	Continuous support, when compared with no doula support, was significantly associated with shorter labors and decreased need for any analgesia, oxytocin, forceps, and C–sections.	*Labor *Birth
Scott, Klaus, & Klaus, 1999	Meta-anlaysis of 12 randomized controlled trials of obstetrical and postpartum outcomes		3 meta-analyses using different approaches performed on the 12 clinical trials.	Doula supported mothers rate childbirth as less difficult and painful. Labor support by fathers does not appear to produce similar perceptions. Eight of 12 trials report reductions in state anxiety scores, positive feelings about birth, and increased breast-feeding initiation. Later benefits include decreased symptoms of depression, improved self-esteem, exclusive breastfeeding, and increased sensitivity of mother to child's needs.	*Newborn *Immediate psychological outcomes *Longer maternal infant outcomes

Continued on next page

Findings From Studies of Labor Support (cont'd)

Study	Method	Participants	Interventions	Outcomes	Benefit Category
Gordon, Walton, McAdam, Derman, Gallitero, & Garrett, 1999	Random assignment to control or experimental group	478 nulliparous women enrolled in a group-model HMO delivering in one of three HMO managed hospitals in California. Experimental group $n=169$, Control group $n=209$.	149 had trained on-call doulas that arrived on patient admission to hospital in labor. 165 had usual routine care without doula support. Phone interviews were conducted at 6 weeks postpartum.	Women who had doulas had significantly less epidural use than usual care group. They were also significantly more likely to rate the experience as good, they coped well in labor, and had positive effect on their perception of bodies strength and performance. No significant difference in C-section, forceps, vacuum, oxytocin, breastfeeding, postpartum depression, or self-esteem measures.	*Labor *Birth *Newborn *Immediate psychological outcomes *Longer term maternal-infant outcomes

Continued on next page

Findings From Studies of Labor Support (cont'd)

Study	Method	Participants	Interventions	Outcomes	Benefit Category
Hodnett, Lowe, Hannah, Willan, Stevens, et al., 2002	Randomized multicenter trial in 13 U.S. and Canadian hospitals	6915 women with singleton or twins, 34 weeks gestation or more and in established labor at randomization	Mothers assigned to: Usual care group n=3461, or continuous support by a specially trained nurse n = 3454 in labor. The purpose was to evaluate the effectiveness of nurses as providers of labor support.	Rate of C-section was 12.5% in continuous care group and 12.6% in usual care group. Women in continuous labor support group less likely to have continuous electronic fetal monitoring. No significant differences in maternal events during labor, birth, or hospital postpartum period. No significant differences in immediate outcomes of infants or breastfeeding. The conclusion of the authors was that "in hospitals characterized by high rates of routine intrapartum interventions, continuous labor support by nurses does not affect the likelihood of cesarean delivery or other medical or psychosocial outcomes of labor and birth."	*Labor *Birth *Newborn

About the Authors

Rachel Abramson, RN, MS, IBCLC, is a maternal–child nurse and a lactation consultant. She was a founder of Chicago Health Connection and has been the executive director since 1989. She was the project director for the 4-year collaborative Chicago Doula Project, originally funded by the Robert Wood Johnson Foundation and the Irving B. Harris Foundation. Rachel has extensive experience in breastfeeding promotion and management, maternal–child health, community-based health services research, community health worker training and nonprofit administration. She is the author of a number of articles on community issues in maternal–child health in national and international journals. In 2003, Rachel received the National Healthy Mothers, Healthy Babies State Impact Award for the Harris Doula Institute at Chicago Health Connection. She was also awarded the Start Early: Learning Begins at Birth Award from Voices for Illinois Children in 2003, and the Harris Award from the ZERO TO THREE Press with a book contract for manuscript development of *The Community-Based Doula: Supporting Families Before, During, and After Childbirth*.

Ginger K. Breedlove, PhD, CNM, ARNP, FACNM, is an assistant professor and director of the Nurse Midwifery Education program at the University of Kansas School of Nursing. Her experience includes co-founding the first freestanding birthing center in Kansas, establishing the first nurse midwifery clinical service in the Greater Kansas City community, and establishing multiple programs caring for underserved populations of women through various federal and state grant awards. She serves as secretary to the American College of Nurse Midwives, Kansas March of Dimes Prematurity Campaign chair, and is on numerous advocacy interest groups related to promoting maternal child health.

Beth Isaacs, BSN, MPH, IBCLC, CD(DONA), received a BS in communicative disorders from Northwestern University in 1976, a BSN from Rush University in 1981, and a MPH from University of Illinois at Chicago in 1998. She has worked as a labor and delivery nurse, childbirth educator, lactation consultant, and lactation educator at Rush University Medical Center since 1980, where she is a complemental faculty member of the College of Nursing. She worked at Chicago Health Connection from 2000 – 2006 as a DONA-certified doula and approved doula trainer. She is the author of a chapter, "Lactation," in *The Textbook of Breast Disease* and the editor of *Sharing our Stories: A Collection Inspired by the First Community-Based Doula Networking Seminar.* She is also the mother of two wonderful daughters.